Elaine, enjoy the read! (handwritten)

THE PRAGMATIST'S GUIDE TO CORPORATE LEAN STRATEGY

Michael Nir (handwritten signature)

INCORPORATING LEAN STARTUP AND LEAN ENTERPRISE PRACTICES IN YOUR BUSINESS

Michael Nir

Apress®

The Pragmatist's Guide to Corporate Lean Strategy: Incorporating Lean Startup and Lean Enterprise Practices in Your Business

Michael Nir
Brookline, Massachusetts, USA

ISBN-13 (pbk): 978-1-4842-3536-2 ISBN-13 (electronic): 978-1-4842-3537-9
https://doi.org/10.1007/978-1-4842-3537-9

Library of Congress Control Number: 2018939160

Managing Director, Apress Media LLC: Welmoed Spahr
Acquisitions Editor: Shiva Ramachandran
Development Editor: Laura Berendson
Coordinating Editor: Rita Fernando

Cover designed by eStudioCalamar

Cover image designed by Freepik (www.freepik.com)

Distributed to the book trade worldwide by Springer Science+Business Media New York, 233 Spring Street, 6th Floor, New York, NY 10013. Phone 1-800-SPRINGER, fax (201) 348-4505, e-mail orders-ny@springer-sbm.com, or visit www.springeronline.com. Apress Media, LLC is a California LLC and the sole member (owner) is Springer Science + Business Media Finance Inc (SSBM Finance Inc). SSBM Finance Inc is a **Delaware** corporation.

For information on translations, please e-mail rights@apress.com, or visit www.apress.com/rights-permissions.

Apress titles may be purchased in bulk for academic, corporate, or promotional use. eBook versions and licenses are also available for most titles. For more information, reference our Print and eBook Bulk Sales web page at www.apress.com/bulk-sales.

Any source code or other supplementary material referenced by the author in this book is available to readers on GitHub via the book's product page, located at www.apress.com/9781484235362. For more detailed information, please visit www.apress.com/source-code.

Printed on acid-free paper

Advance praise for *The Pragmatist's Guide to Corporate Lean Strategy*

"Michael has demystified 'simplification' with this in-depth review of lean. Each chapter is easy to implement with research and best practices presented so there is a direct translation to applicability for corporate entities."

—Matt Brooks, Vice President,
Data and Analytics Culture Transformation, GE

"Michael Nir walks you through corporate lean strategy in a step-by-step manner so you can be successful in today's constantly changing and complex world. Tips, best practices, and anti-patterns show you direction, while mini-stories of success and failure of an enterprise lean agile transformation provide a reality check."

—Zuzana (Zuzi) Sochova, Agile and Enterprise Coach;
Certified Scrum Trainer; Author of *The Great ScrumMaster Book*;
Board member, Scrum Alliance

"Michael Nir boils down advanced concepts into a framework that can be used to evolve organizations, independent of their size, so you can transform an organization into a customer-centric organization."

—Klas Skogmar, Entrepreneur
and Management Consultant, Arkatay Consulting

"Michael explains the differences between adopting lean/agile ways of working in small and medium organizations vs. the more complex dynamics of enterprises with 500-plus people. He teaches how to overcome challenges and successfully turn a corporate 'oil tanker' into a nimble 'flotilla,' all working together toward a common goal."

—Shane Hastie,
Director of Agile Learning Programs at ICAgile

"I always ask myself whether a book is 'readable,' 'referenceable,' 'relevant,' and 'realistic.' (I have a personal issue with pure theory unproven by real-life experience). In the case of this book, the answers are all a loud 'Yes.'"

—Peter Taylor, Head of Global PMO at Aptos Retail

"Michael Nir synthesizes the five essential elements for a lean agile transformation; explains how they differ when applied to organizations that are not startups; and provides a concrete timeline for a successful lean agile transformation."

—Yuan Cheng, SVP, Engineering at Everbridge

"I've seen this approach first hand, and it works. If you're an executive, leader, or practitioner and you want to make sure you're building the right product, this book is for you."

—Richard Kasperowski, Speaker, Trainer, Coach, and Author focused on high-performance teams

"In this book Michael Nir asks critical questions for leaders to consider when managing innovation. This must-read guide extends the findings of Ries' *The Lean Startup* by getting to the root of what drives innovation and how leaders tick. Not only does the author consider why leaders in organizations should innovate, he also provides nuts-and-bolts advice on how they can optimize their practices to encourage innovation in the organization so the organization can be an innovation leader."

—Dr. Gail Ferreira, Innovation Lean-Agile Leader

"As a veteran of five startups and three multi-billion dollar companies, I know that a 10,000 person company is more than just 100 startups stuck together. Michael Nir understands this. In his book, he shows you how to deal with the reality that as companies grow, they develop a culture that is deeply embedded in their hierarchy. He presents a framework and specific techniques for breaking through the resistance and installing a mindset of experimentation and learning. He provides examples from his personal experience that show how to stay true to the principles of lean startup combined with the agile mindset, design thinking, and Lean UX and overcome challenges during your organization's enterprise-wide agile journey."

—David Grabel, Enterprise Agile Coach, Treasurer and Former President of Agile New England

"Michael Nir is a first-class lean agile coach who has written a practical guide and clearly articulates theory while diving into tangible examples and stories from his field of work. Executives at any large organization will want to read this book as it covers all the major challenges organizations face and provides tangible guidance, with examples, data, and theory to back it up. After working with Michael for many years, I can attest to his success and credibility as a brilliant coach who always puts organizational results first."

—Zubin Irani, Founder and CEO of cPrime, Inc., an Alten Group Company

"This book is a must-read for anyone interested in succeeding at organizational improvement. I've been in several situations where in hindsight I wish I could have gift this book to the decision makers leading their organization's transformation journey. You won't regret reading this book."

—Scott Ambler, Fellow, Disciplined Agile Consortium, Co-Author, An Executive's Guide to Disciplined Agile: Winning the Race to Business Agility

To all those still searching for their true calling.

Contents

About the Author

Michael Nir is a keynote speaker, bestselling author, and Lean Agile Inspiration Expert, known for his passion, creativity, and innovation.

His Masters in Engineering, certification in Project Management, and training in gestalt balance his technical know-how with emotional intelligence. He inspires people and teams to change, experientially and emotionally, while climbing the hill AND reaching the summit.

The author of nine books on influence, consumer experience, and agile project management, Michael delivers practical skills gained from 18 years of experience leading change at global organizations in diverse industries such as Intel, Philips Healthcare, United Healthcare, DnB, Volvo, JPMorgan Chase, Citi, Unilever, and many others. He is masterful at connecting the dots between human behavior, business systems, and work environment to drive highly productive teams and lead individuals to communicate effectively.

Michael draws on unique personal experiences that provide him with valuable insight. During college in Israel, he led groups of adolescents on excursions through the desert, observing natural leadership behaviors in team settings. Later, on a hike to Alaska, he had to face down a 250-pound grizzly bear, giving him a dramatic taste of what it's like to influence a powerful and threatening personality using wits alone.

Michael was born in Los Angeles and resides in Boston. He travels extensively to Europe and East Asia to provide consulting and facilitating training. He understands people, organizations, and cultures and is comfortable leading cross-functional and cross-cultural workshops.

A passionate guide and mentor for organizations undergoing change, he has also developed lean startup training and delivery programs as well as gestalt team-building and conflict management workshops.

You can reach Michael at his website (http://michaelnir.com/) and by email at m.nir@sapir-cs.com.

Foreword

Software has eaten the world, and now the pace of technological change is eating companies that try to operate without a lean mindset. Large enterprises must transform to compete and thrive in the modern digital economy. This requires operating with a lean mindset from top to bottom and side to side to keep up with the rapidly accelerating pace of change. A transformation of this magnitude is daunting for even the world's most admired companies because the required shift in mindset, culture, and practice impacts the entire organization. So how do you go from business as usual to a technology-enabled disruptor that can rapidly adapt and respond?

Michael answers one of the hardest questions executives and transformation leaders face in the modern economy: Where do I begin my journey to enterprise agility? He brings together the best of lean startup, scaled agile, Lean UX, design thinking, and DevOps, distilling the most important principles into 30-day, 90-day, and 1-year guides to help you focus on customers from the onset, communicate your vision, synthesize an operating model, measure what truly matters, and take steps to pivot while preserving what works.

Michael explains the keys to success: falling in love with the challenge, not the problem; fostering an environment of enterprise agility; and rapidly learning via lean experiments that drive transformation to build a corporate machine that innovates like a startup. Michael's use of lean analogies and anti-patterns, combined with his in-depth knowledge and experience in the field of transformation, make his book a great read for every executive, software leader, and transformation expert responsible for leading change in large corporation.

—Steve Elliot
Founder and CEO of Agilecraft

Acknowledgments

This book would have been published by my company, Sapir Consulting US, like I've done nine times before if not for Mariya Breyter who, inspired by my prior books, encouraged me to write a book summarizing my experience with lean agile strategy and implementation. This was an autumn Friday in October 2017. By Sunday, Mariya shared the proposal with Shiva from Apress. The end result you are holding in your hands. We spent many hours on video discussing the approach for this book. Thank you, Mariya, for your family's patience during those long weekend sessions and for your inspiration, innovative feedback, and creative ideas.

When we started collaborating, we actually had a comic book in mind. While that is still out and about (you can view the progress in my newsletter), my spouse's graphical and drawing skills for the book you're reading have been instrumental in providing clarity where words are mute. All drawings in this book were created by her. Thanks, Chen, for the creativity, encouragement, and love. Your art is impactful and inspiring and your true calling.

To the Apress team, Shiva, Rita, and Laura, thanks for providing clarity, supporting me through the process, and making this book a reality; the fast iterative feedback is truly agile and the quick validation is the essence of lean.

After many years abroad, I arrived in Boston a day after the mega-storm of February 2015 to lay the groundwork for homecoming. I had never been to the city before, except for a fleeting drive-through when I was eight years old. Snow piled up into seven-foot-high banks and all was at a standstill. This didn't stop Richard Kasperwoski from meeting with me downtown for lunch and sharing thoughts about agile, the core protocols, gestalt, and more. Richard welcomed me in a way that still moves me. Thanks, Richard, for opening your heart; your kindness has truly touched me and impacted my predisposition to business relationships from which a true friendship blossomed.

That same snowy morning, John Todd from PMI Massbay and Downtown recruiting invited me for a coffee and shared his thoughts about opportunities in the city for an agile expert who just landed. John, your insights and nuggets were highly valuable. Thanks!

Training and coaching lean startup in a non-software enterprise was the result of collaboration with a large insurance company in Indianapolis. Scott McClintic, I don't have many opportunities to co-facilitate. The lean startup workshops we ideated, structured, and facilitated together were valuable and lots of fun. You were the first one to ask where I got the clunky accent and did some research to verify that. I value your perspective and comradery. And I finally learned what an Arnold Palmer is. Relearning how to scale agile with remote teams and tie lean thinking to human-centric design and lean UX in an insurance provider was a journey and there is still more headway to make. John, Doug, Jeff, Jeremy, Ben, Graham, Liz, Sue, and Vijay, we have a long way ahead of us; in the face of digital disruption, we must transform our thinking and deliver the right results faster.

Liza and the cPrime team, the agile and lean training and coaching engagements provided me with perspective, ideas and many stories. cPrime is an amazing company and it's great collaborating with you.

To the Constant Contact team (Ken, Piyum, Jim, Wendy, Sue, Bob and Bob, Damon, Susan, Amanda, Raj, Keith, Arnis, Chris, Gene, and many others), thanks for creating an amazing and stimulating startup-like work environment. I've learned a lot about how agile, Lean UX, innovation labs, scaling, continuous delivery, continuous integration, and OPS should operate together and the challenges in making it work.

Ben Ho, our luncheons in the city where we discuss startups, lean, agile, scaling, software, mobile, and food are an inspiration—gastronomical, cognitive, and cultural.

In March of 2014 I met Henrik Kniberg in Helsingborg, Sweden. We were both speaking at the Swedish Passion for Projects conference. We spent the morning before our talks strolling around the old city and sharing ideas and thoughts. I wasn't aware at the time of who Henrik was and his impact on practical Scrum coaching, and I think he kind of liked it that way. I am delighted that I was ignorant since his practical, matter of fact approach to agile coaching and the way he presented his thoughts impacted my coaching style profusely. Thanks, Henrik.

My daughter's teacher asked the class how many of them don't understand their parents' occupation. A third of the class raised their hands, my daughter included. The truth is I am not sure myself. I like Dean Leaffingwell's answer; he defines himself as a lifelong learner. But that's just evading the question. Maybe this book will provide you a partial answer. I do know, Tal and Rotem, that whoever I am and whatever work I pursue, I am guided by love. Raising children is a lean startup with some human-centric design, consumer focus, and lots of agility. Yes, you can read the books; however, none really prepare you, since parenting is about assumptions, validations, and pivoting. It has been quite a ride so far and I'm looking forward to the years to come, together.

Next time they ask, tell them that your dad is a mountain biker. It'll save you the trouble.

Preface: Cadence Is King

Writing about lean strategy and execution in the enterprise is for me a closing of a circle. In the summer of 2005, I was completing my Masters degree in industrial engineering and taking my first steps as an independent consultant. I was residing in the northern part of Israel, and I was helping local production plants focus on value, eliminate waste in process, and implement Kanban systems. Among my clients were Delmar-Industries, a water control solutions manufacturer; Cabiran, an innovative aluminum casting solution manufacturer; and Milopri, a fruit packing plant for exports.

The two projects that stand out the most were both improvement projects done for Delmar-Industries. Delmar-Industries are experts in water flow management. They design, manufacture, and supply products and solutions to enhance and protect water systems in waterworks, irrigation, buildings, mining, and fire protection.

The first Delmar project had to do with efficiency improvement at a large metal color-coating manufacturing line. The other Delmar project was a lean production physical layout and Kanban system implementation with elements of change transformation since it included two rival groups of Kibbutz members in two adjacent production facilities with a history of discord dating to the founding of Kibbutz Genofar.

It is the first project done in Kibbutz Ein-Debi that I want to share with you, since it really stumped me. The building that housed the large metal-parts color-coating production line was like a complex maze. The metal parts were hung from above on a slow-moving conveyor belt by a team of three. The parts then went into preheating. The core part of the system was color-coating; two employees sprayed the parts using spray guns. Next, the parts went into a curing oven and later into low heat. The last step was unmounting the parts from the conveyor belt and placing them in an orderly fashion on the finished good inventory, ready to be transferred to the next assembly lines.

We were a team of three: Michelle, a bright industrial engineering under graduate who later graduated from INSEAD business school, a part-time intern doing mostly statistical sampling, and myself. As is common for industrial engineering engagements, the problem that we were out to solve was improving efficiency; needless to add that the 20 employees that worked in shifts didn't eye us approvingly. The kickoff meeting was accompanied with mutual suspicion: the employees weren't excited to have a team of snotty engineers perform a time study in their production line and meddle in their production line kingdom, and we were concerned with the level of cooperation of the team and how to make sure they wouldn't rig the system. To foster trust, we received the VP of Operations and the CEOs guarantee that no jobs will be impacted as a result of the project.

We spent the first month learning the production process, analyzing the sequencing, going through three years' worth of historical data, and performing a time study; we found out very little. There were hundreds of different parts in various sizes and shapes, and the weights of the parts varied dramatically from several pounds to thousands of pounds. Three standard coating colors were applied: green for agriculture, blue for city waterworks, and red for fire protection, the latter of which required the most care. The time taken to preheat and then cure each part was in relation to size and functionality. Switching from colors was a time-consuming ordeal and required scheduling in advance the daily production order. Performing a time study in this complex environment was excruciating and we gained very little understanding as to the average time for a part to go through the entire line.

We quickly understood that the critical step was the manual work of color-coating the metal parts. There were six painters rotating in two shifts, with differing levels of expertise. Considering the possible combinations among painter skillset and experience, part size, shape, weight and color, heating and curing pattern, and switching colors, the problem of identifying the "correct" throughput rate of the production line based on the time for color-coating was intractable. The average time to color-coat ranged from 60 seconds to 8 minutes. On top of which, the painters accelerated and decelerated the speed of the conveyor belt based on their completion rate, curing time, color, shape, and how hot the black coffee was that they were sipping. We were stumped by the magnitude of the problem. The solution eluded us for weeks and we needed inspiration.

I remember sitting with Michelle observing the color-coating process at 10 p.m. on a Sunday night and together trying to formulate the problem we were witnessing. We decided to just observe the painters performing their job, without judging, counting, measuring, and thinking about a solution. We also spent time with the employees: we shared coffee and tea, we shared jokes and stories, and we learned more about the routine work of the color-coating manufacturing line. We were learning into what is known as the "unmeasurables." Thus we observed for a day, and then a week, and a month. Michelle asked me to what end were we observing; back then I couldn't articulate an answer, and yet I knew that by viewing the work where it is performed without being judgmental of the process and the employees, a solution would emerge.

And then, after a month of intermittent observations we noticed a pattern in the data, and the solution dawned on us. Once we had seen it, the answer was very simple; however, it was so counterintuitive that we had to vet it for a month before we presented it to the executives.

When engineers set to solve a problem of efficiency, or for that matter, any person that is set to tackle a problem of efficiency, they usually focus on accomplishing more or work faster. That's true for almost any problem of efficiency, and there are many such problems that are similar in nature: how can I study faster, how can I complete my tasks faster so I finish the work day and head home, how can I go faster through my emails, how can I complete shopping faster, which is the faster route through traffic, how do I add more features on a product, how do I get more likes on my page, and so on. We measure the time to complete the task and ask ourselves how can we increase time or decrease costs.

However, we often miss the holistic nature of the environment we operate in. We are primed for these problems from a very young age, so we rarely look at the non-work time, the time that we are not engaged in the task; still, the fact remains that most opportunities for increasing the rate of completion or throughput are by addressing the non-work time—the waste. In Japan, where lean thinking originated, they call this non-required work process step *muda*.

During her observations Michelle noticed something odd; that while the painters' direct working time was rather erratic, the combined non-work time for the two painters was complimentary to the work time and both were consistent and a constant. Thus, regardless of the many variables, the combined value of both times across all products could be articulated easily.

We both knew the value of one piece flow and Takt time; both are lean manufacturing concepts that have later been adapted to agile project management. Takt time, or cadence, is the average time between the start of production of one unit and the start of production of the next unit. These production times are set to match the rate of customer demand. Our problem was how to define the cadence for the coloring production line with the various moving parts and the internal consumer demand. Now we had an answer, a simple solution that was hard to accept and counterintuitive. I mentioned previously that the average time to color-coat ranged from 60 seconds to 8 minutes. We analyzed the data and noticed that the parts taking more than 7 minutes were outliers and occurred only when the coffee was too hot or due to external impacts. Actually, most parts were colored in 2 to 5 minutes. However, the perception of the painters was that they were working very hard all the time, which was true since they were missing a constant rhythm. They didn't have a sense of a beat; rather the parts kept coming erratically and they were frantically keeping up. This impacted the entire line since there was no consistent flow.

So what if we slowed the line for all the parts to 6 minutes? Reflect about that for a moment. What are the benefits accomplished by identifying a constant rate? Naturally it brings order to a chaotic system; it allows all the employees to plan around a consistent order and flow. I mentioned that the production line was like a maze; by introducing cadence to the system, the employees could now experience the same flow without seeing one another. We could mount clocks with counters that showed the progress of the cadence. It was truly revolutionary. It was bringing order from chaos.

Naturally the painters and others employees in the production line were ecstatic; we'd actually given them permission to work slower, or rather, work relaxed. The line managers and the VP of Operations were happy to have predictability. That said, we needed to persuade the color-coating department manager to make the change since it impacted his operations. On top of all, the executive leaders were happy. Overall completion rate was improved by 23% without any capital investment. The definition of a cadence also impacted upstream incoming inventory and downstream production; other centers of the factory could align to the cadence and thus inventory levels could be reduced since the constant rhythm reduced jitter or randomness. Last but not least, while traditionally, assigning direct labor standard-cost-per part is tricky, specifically when each part has its own color coating duration and there are thousands of variants, our solution made standard-part-cost pricing effortless since all parts had the same direct labor cost. Talk about a win-win solution!

Michelle and I were perplexed to see the result unfold before our eyes and were surprised to see how simple the solution had been.

I learned a crucial lesson from that project: always search for the simple solution. Often that solution is hidden in plain sight. It is within reach; however, it requires asking the right questions and moving away from traditional assumptions. Less is often more and cadence is king.

Later on I found that this is a recurring pattern for successful consulting engagements.

Introduction: Microwave Thinking

It's all in the microwave: the problem, the needs, the decisions, the product solution, and the waste, the incredible waste.

Do you own a microwave?

You probably do.

Take a short trip to your kitchen and have a look.

How many buttons are on your microwave's keypad? How many features does it offer? How many pre-preprogrammed options are available?

Now, honestly, how many do you actually use?

If you are like most people that I've met, you probably use two or three, four max.

Most people readily admit to using just one button. I'm guilty of the same; I place the food-loaded plate onto the revolving dish, close the door, and without hesitation press the 1-minute cook button.

Sometimes I'll hit it three, four, or ten times, depending on what I'm heating, basing my decision on trial and error, or in other words, previous times I used the appliance.

I know that there's a specific button for cooking a sweet potato and another for meat and yet another for soup. I read the instructions at one point and actually tried the features out, but I just can't remember if pressing the button once cooks a single sweet potato that weighs between 10 to 15 ounces or maybe it is for two sweet potatoes? Who cares? I just want a cooked meal, and so, like so many others, I'll hit the one-minute fast cooking button a couple of times and hope for the best.

Based on feedback I've received in numerous presentations and workshops I delivered, I think I am in good company. Many of us don't really care about the plethora of features our microwave offers.

We buy them, but we don't use them the way they are engineered to be used.

Don't even get me started about universal remotes. If you are over 20 years old, you'll remember those gigantic devices with over 115 buttons. How I yearned for a universal remote that controlled, from a single device, all the remote-controlled electronics in our living room.

Go back even further in time,. Remember the option-loaded VCR that befuddled our attempts to program it to record our favorite TV show weekly at 7:30 PM for 50 minutes?

There's a recurring pattern that emerges as we examine the devices that we gingerly purchase and then live with. We pay for many functions that we don't use on most of the appliances. They are usually over-engineered. Don't be fooled, though; it is not an engineering problem, it is a business challenge.

This is wasteful!

■ **Tip**   Review Figure I-1. How many buttons are on your microwave? Can you assign the features to the buttons? If you can't name all of them, it is a hint that too many features are offered. Use this approach with products that you offer.

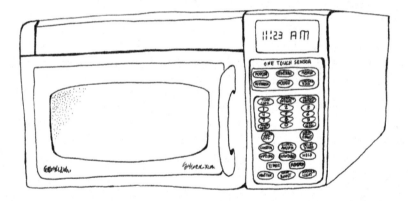

Figure I-1. How many buttons are on your microwave? (Source: Graphic design by Hen Nir. © Sapir Consulting US LLC 2017, www.michaelnir.com)

It is wasteful to engineering, to production, to the business, to the consumer, and above all to the environment! We all pay for this waste.

Whose fault is it?

Looking for fault within the business usually goes like this:

Engineering blames product research and marketing for not nailing the right requirements for the product.

Product development blames engineering for spending too much time creating the optimal solution, over-engineering the solution, and missing the deadlines.

Marketing blames product development for messing up with the consumer and meddling in the marketing turf.

Operations blames marketing and engineering for delivering unsupportable products and sales for selling them.

And sales, they blame everyone.

At the end of the day, it's those low-paid consumer reps that have to deal with the aftermath of the overly complex widgets that are sold.

On top of all, the businesses always blame the consumer—for not knowing what they want, for not using it the way they should, for not reading the manual, and for generally being stupid.

One common joke among business leaders is that if we didn't have those pesky customers, our products would be great.

I once worked with a software shop that created email marketing tools to analyze the return on investment for features it delivered. The analysis validated existing research: approximately 60 to 70% of the features were not used. In other words, they wasted about 70% of their engineering and product development capacity. To put it bluntly, the company could have fired 70% of its 500 engineers and still appreciate the same revenue for that year. This thinking, however, is deceptive, since we never know which of the features would be revenue generating and which wouldn't.

And we weren't stupid. When we crafted the strategy and decided which features would be developed, we were convinced that the ones we selected were the right ones; we focused on the features that would win us the market.

We didn't say, "Hey, let's select some features that we know are wasteful just because we have engineering capacity."

That would have been ludicrous.

We were not stupid, and people are not stupid. People and companies don't create features just for the gist of it. Often, there is a lengthy, tedious, time-consuming process for vetting the features that the company will develop, and yet two-thirds of the time the people and the business are wrong.

Actually, if you ask people at your workplace for the one feature that would be THE game changer for your company, you would receive numerous responses. People provide ideas easily but most of them would be wrong! It is a humbling experience.

This problem between what we, the employees, leaders, and managers, think will be the "killer feature" and what actually creates value from a consumer perspective is difficult to accept.

I was sharing the research and my experience with the senior leadership of a software company. The CEO listened intently and then shared his point of view. He told me, "Look, this is all very nice. I sit on many boards of software companies in the Boston area. I agree; there are many stupid board members that I have to live with. But," he added, "We are different. We are smarter. We are not like the rest of the software companies in the Boston area. We are able to identify the features that we'll need, develop them, and win the market. The data even supports it!" Later, after I concluded the session, the senior vice president of product approached me. He shared that he verifies that the data always supports the decisions in retrospect, by hiding the feature decisions that were wrong…

By now I hope that you agree with the premise that *we, the people, create stuff we never use.*

Since this challenge is known, have there have been efforts to solve it?

How have companies been approaching the issue of developing the features that we don't need?

Usually without much success!

Traditionally, businesses tried a catch-all approach of *develop whatever you can and hope for the best.* It worked for some time when consumers didn't have a choice or access to the Internet; presently it is a surefire method to go out of business.

Another approach was and still is known as *the enlightened leader.* The senior leaders by virtue of their position, experience, and intelligence dictate the strategy and features that need to be developed. They were and still are wrong two-thirds of the times, but nobody tells them.

Technology companies adopt agile development and a slew of other approaches in order to align the developed product with the consumer needs.

They treat agile as a silver bullet without recognizing the limits of agile delivery approaches. They invest in engineering and product delivery, hire coaches and Scrum Masters, and achieve little business impact. Yes, agile helps in speeding the engineering development effort and responding to change; however, faster engineering means that we make the same feature mistakes, yet deliver them faster to the market. In other words, agile doesn't necessarily remove the feature development waste.

Another approach to solving the mismatch between the features the business delivers and what the consumer needs is design thinking. Design thinking instructs us to interact with the consumer following a five-step method.

One of the manifestations of design thinking can be seen in the proliferation of innovation labs. They ideate features based on consumer needs and create beautiful designs; however, they tend to be segregated from the business. The concept is worthy; however, the implementations are often subpar. The disconnect between the innovation lab's lofty ideas and the product delivery organization frequently make the labs a waste of time, resources, and effort.

Lean UX and UX Strategy try to connect feature delivery and the consumer need, but fall short of achieving it because they are often perceived as an external application of ideas to the core product delivery structure and fail to harness the support of operations, sales, and marketing.

Scaled Agile is trying to be an all-inclusive, one-stop shop, a framework that includes the entire organization; however having its roots in software development, it has a limit in its breadth and has so far been limited in its ability to impact business agility.

Marketing organizes focused groups, runs surveys, and immerses itself in market research; however, they focus on the wrong tools and thus receive the wrong answers since, at heart, we are of a different mindset when we shop for an item and when we use the item. When marketing conducts a focus group for gathering requirements, people are asked about what they want, not what they need. When we are queried, many of us think we want a microwave with lots of options, yet that's not the way we use the appliance. I suggest that if we built microwaves based on their usage, the appliance would appear different. Can you think what it might offer that's different?

Make no mistake; the challenge is not limited to software development. The problem of delivering the wrong feature set is rampant in insurance, banking, automotive, financial, leisure, and other industries.

So, what now? Is it even possible to meet customer needs when the customers themselves generally do not know what they need until they try it out? And even if we do, the world is changing more rapidly than many companies can even build their products. In the era of digital disruption, high customer expectations, and commitment to quality, how can an enterprise of a significant size survive the uncertainty of the business landscape, market demand-related high customer expectations, and produce the products that customers need fast, with excellence, and at scale?

If anyone says that there is a "one solution fits all" answer, they would be unrealistic. However, over years working with multiple enterprises in different industries and observing multiple successes and failures, I noticed that there are patterns that succeed across industries and cultures, and there are anti-patterns that force companies to backslide and lose to the competition. I have been searching for the right sequence for these patterns, and I have synthesized five steps that have universal significance. These patterns are not unknown to the world. They utilize lean, agile, design thinking, lean startup values, and principles in a structured methodical way, allowing for predictable outcomes in an uncertain business environment. We can use these patterns to create an ecosystem that allows enterprises to rapidly respond to the changing environment while maintaining their historic strengths and market presence.

In this book, I am going to share with you the framework that allows for flexibility of response to the market while maximizing the brand and scale. You are probably wondering how this is possible given the legacy thinking, frequently hierarchical culture, and cost of running an existing business, and you are right. It is extremely difficult.

To explain how is this possible, I'll use an example from software design. By having a modular software architecture, we are able to reuse and maximize the use of software components, as well as retire those that are no longer needed without any impact to the whole ecosystem. A former colleague, who leads one of engineering departments for a health insurance giant, used a great example of a cruise ship vs. a speedboat. It's hard to steer a cruise ship because it's huge and heavy and takes a lot of time and effort to gain momentum. If you have many speed boats with advanced communication mechanisms, you can point as many of them as needed in any direction that is required, as long as they have an ability to align and return back to base to recharge and get ready for the next highest priority task.

Similarly, the framework that I am sharing with you in this book is modular and component-based. Each chapter defines the sequence and the nature of each components, as well as provides implementation examples for companies of different sizes and industries.

My intent in writing this book is to describe the required successful foundation for linking collaborative innovation, cultural transformation, and product execution in the context of true business agility.

Start with Why

Getting Ready for Transformation

The first chapter in this book is Chapter Zero. This naming convention is frequently used in Scrum, one of the agile frameworks, which emphasizes team-based, value-driven, incremental delivery. In order to deliver consistent value, the team needs to ensure that the prerequisites are met: goals and success criteria are defined and shared, the product backlog (prioritized list of deliverables) is established, the cross-functional execution team is available, and everyone is clear on their roles and expectations. There is also a delivery framework in place—agile, lean, or lean startup—that will be followed by the team and the identified stakeholders. The combination of team norms and rules is referred to as a "working agreement."

I decided to "eat my own dog food" and start this book with a Chapter Zero to align with you on your expectations, my deliverables within the book, and our joint "working agreement."

A helpful way of introducing a change to the organization is to start by answering simple questions: Why? (What is the ultimate goal we'd like to achieve?), What? (What is the change we want to introduce?), and How? (How are we going to do this?). You can frame any conversation about the change at any level to make it inspirational and compelling to your audience. I am going to use this technique to introduce my book to you so that you can add it to your toolbox, whether you want to inspire your team, align on the approach, or get buy-in from senior management.

In his book *Start with Why*,[1] Simon Sinek suggests that the primary goal of inspiring others is to provide a compelling vision. Following the suggestion above, let's start with Why?

Why Did I Write This Book and Who Is It For?

My goal, based on my experience with transforming enterprises and enabling them to survive in a modern, highly disruptive business environment, is to enable you to envision, plan, and orchestrate this transition. I provide a framework that you can follow in order to achieve success in building an adaptive, value-driven environment of high-performance teams of motivated practitioners who produce results that delight their customers. Based on excellent underlying models, frameworks, and mindsets (lean, agile, the startup way, Lean UX, design thinking, DEVOPS, 4DX, and other adjacent concepts), this approach brings it all together by providing a concise and verified framework that you can follow in implementing positive change in your organization.

The audience of this book includes anyone who is interested in this concept, because everyone is an actor in the enterprise change.

These groups will benefit from the ideas expressed in this book:

- The CEO of the company, who is the sponsor of any major change initiative and who has a vested interest in enabling the company to survive disruption from the market or from its own customers whose preferences change on a daily basis;

- An enterprise-level change agent or leader (enterprise leaders, transformation coaches, and other professionals whose job is to orchestrate the transformation);

- Any employee of the company who is either an early adopter of the change or resists this change because of job security considerations, any other fear, or who genuinely believes that things are going well and there is nothing to change;

- A customer who has a vested interest in resulting outcome.

In sum, everyone is a stakeholder of the enterprise transformation and determines collectively the success of it.

---

[1]Simon Sinek, *Start with Why: How Great Leaders Inspire Everyone to Take Action* (New York, NY: Portfolio, 2011).

"Survival is not compulsory. Improvement is not compulsory, but improvement is necessary for survival."

—W. Edwards Deming, Statistician and leading management thinker in the field of quality[2]

Having a consistent and relevant framework of organizational change and improving it on an ongoing basis is a prerequisite of survival for an enterprise and is a prerequisite for building the products that customers need. Disruptions happen in modern business on a daily basis, and it is only a matter of a few years before a disruption gets disrupted by a new one. Consider the experience of paper maps being replaced by GPS devices only to be replaced by similar smartphone functionality within a few years.

There have been many books written about this topic but none that I am aware of provide a clear step-by-step framework allowing the readers to succeed in the fast-paced, customer-centric, value-oriented environment the world experiences today.

As shared above, I started with a "why" following Simon Sinek's famous approach, which is part of every organizational transformation. Similar to Simon Sinek, I will talk about why some companies achieve things that completely exceed customer expectations, defying all our assumptions for what's possible, and why some fail despite their prior unquestionable success. There has been a lot written about why companies like Facebook, Amazon, Apple, and Google achieved extraordinary results while Kodak, Blockbuster, and Borders are not in business anymore. While I recognize that the latter companies failed to inspire, provide compelling vision, meet customer needs, and respond to the market, I will test these and similar failures within my model to share a holistic view and organizational transformation timing, needs, success, and failures through these experiences.

Now that I have shared my vision on why such book is needed, let's talk about "What?"

What Is This Book About?

I will start by describing what this book is not about:

- It is not about the eight phases of change, although it follows John Kotter's leading change model.[3]

---

[2]Institute for Enterprise Excellence (IEX), Mike Stoecklein, "Side (by Side) Management," http://instituteforexcellence.org/wp-content/uploads/2017/07/side-by-side-mgmt-5-1-17-v1.pdf, July, 2017.
[3]John Kotter, *Leading Change*, (Watertown, MA: Harvard Business Review Press, 2012).

- It is not about the agile approach and the Scrum method to deliver team-based results as per Sutherland in *Scrum: The Art of Doing Twice the Work in Half the Time.*[4]

- It is not about the scaled agile approach to scaling agile delivery, mostly IT, software and hardware product teams as per Dean Leffingwell.[5]

- It not about entrepreneurial management in driving organizational growth as in *The Startup Way* by Eric Ries.[6]

- It is not about disciplined execution as described in *The 4 Disciplines of Execution: Achieving Your Wildly Important Goals* by Sean Covey and Chris McChesney.[7]

- It is not about the organizational culture change leading to a successful agile transformation, as described by Mario Moreira.[8]

- Finally, it is not about IT aspect of digital transformation in creating a lean enterprise—a high performance organization innovating at scale.[9]

And yet, in some way, it is about all of it. So why write another book after all these excellent books have been published and the concepts above have been widely shared?

To answer this question, let me share a story from a consulting experience.

While working for a large airline company, I admired the customer-centric attitude, family-like atmosphere, and the intrinsic motivation that governed the company throughout almost 50 years of existence. There was no difficulty getting buy-in to do things in a new way, which is required to survive tough market and economic challenges; the challenges were about creating consistent practices across the organization, whether it was relevant to product envisioning, marketing, sales, or software test automation.

---

[4]Jeff Sutherland and JJ Sutherland, *Scrum: The Art of Doing Twice the Work in Half the Time* (New York, NY: Currency, 2014).
[5]Dean Leffingwell, *SAFe® 4.0 Reference Guide: Scaled Agile Framework® for Lean Software and Systems Engineering* (Boston, MA: Addison-Wesley Professional, 2016).
[6]Eric Ries, *The Startup Way: How Modern Companies Use Entrepreneurial Management to Transform Culture and Drive Long-Term Growth*, (New York, NY: Currency, 2017).
[7]Chris McChesney, Sean Covey, and Jim Huling, *The 4 Disciplines of Execution: Achieving Your Wildly Important Goals* (New York, NY: Free Press, 2016).
[8]Mario Moreira, *The Agile Enterprise: Building and Running Agile Organizations* (New York, NY: Apress, 2017).
[9]Barry O'Reilly, Jez Humble, and Joanne Molesky, *Lean Enterprise: How High Performance Organizations Innovate at Scale* (Hoboken, NJ: O'Reilly, 2015).

For this type of open culture, the top-down disciplined approach attempted by a group of external consultants would have an immediate negative impact on employee morale and customer experience. The best approach, which was chosen by the company, was to elicit structure from within while sharing and evangelizing best practices. As simple as it sounds, this approach was immediately stalled by the need to identify tools and mechanisms for internal communication and experience sharing, consistent scaling practices at program and enterprise level, templates for product development, customer satisfaction analysis, common metrics, internal communication including social media, wikis and common repositories, and alignment on shared understanding of goals and measures of success.

There were multiple products envisioning and innovation workshops going on, but none of them resulted in a new product or service. Multiple departments started implementing an agile framework to build a solid delivery pipeline but failed to scale or align on timelines and dependences. Customer-facing groups started implementing product envisioning and feedback techniques. Proactive managers initiated innovation workshops. Everyone started their own customer outreach on top of traditionally strong customer satisfaction practices. This enthusiasm contributed to more chaos.

Confused employees requested training on new methods of customer feedback, which was not yet developed. Department leaders were stepping on each other toes and competing to develop innovative strategies in silos. With all the right intentions and correct approach, the company leadership delivered on the shared vision, enthusiasm, and support, and failed to deliver on orchestrating next steps: scaling approach, creating playbooks, templates, tools, techniques—all the aspects required to execute a successful enterprise transformation.

This is where the need for a single-source playbook, simple and pragmatic, became obvious. There are many excellent books on almost every aspect of modern organizational transformation—agile and lean culture and leadership, IT practices, product envisioning and design, with the latest interest in "business agility" as it relates to finance, marketing, people practices, and other adjacent areas. My experience is that many practitioners are inspired by these books and start implementing these practices without assessing the impact they have on others: agile teams develop code without marketing readiness, or the product evangelists creating product portfolio in collaboration with customers without being backed up by finance. Fortunately, the airline leaders in this example were quickly able to identify and implement a holistic transformation approach that resulted in multiple service wins and compressed timelines.

This book contains step-by-step guidance along with the stories from multiple companies I worked with, from health insurance to financial services, media, and education. I share compelling stories and lessons learned from their journeys and my hands-on experience. I share the timelines to help you decide on realistic and feasible expectations vs. demands of "go faster" from senior leaders, which is one of the primary reasons why enterprise transformation fails. I review other reasons of value and signs of success, which enable you in evaluating your own lean enterprise implementation.

When you complete reading this book, you will be well equipped to make your organizational lean adoption a success. You will be able to define the strategy, get buy-in from internal stakeholders, partner with your customer effectively, and reduce business risk via validated learning. The concept of entrepreneurial mindset in a corporate level won't seem an oxymoron to you anymore and the new way of thinking will become part of your daily work routine, no matter your role in the enterprise. This will lead to business success as well as career development—all on top of customer delight and collaborative mindset. Win-win for everyone!

Anti-Pattern   I have been reading various publications equating a pragmatic corporate lean strategy to a lean startup adoption, basically claiming that enterprise is similar to a startup, just bigger, and that in order to succeed one merely has to scale the thinking and scale the same patterns learned from startups to corporates. I couldn't disagree more. Essentially, this is like saying that the thinking patterns of a 3-year-old toddler are the same as a 23-year-old person.

Enterprises, corporations, and, generally speaking, organizations with more than 500 employees are inherently different than startups. When growing, organizations transform, undergoing something like a chemical reaction. Thus a big organization is not a mix of the total number of employees, rather it is a compound. One can't separate the elements back and create multiple lean startups; it is destined to fail. Rather, one must approach the corporate lean strategy pragmatically from the perspective of a chemist, figuring out the ingredients that interact with the organizational compound required to create the necessary change in culture, behaviors, and patterns. I aim to provide these ingredients in this book.

Get Into the Entrepreneurial Mindset

Change Leaders as Entrepreneurs

The goal of this book is to equip you, the reader, with everything you need to build these products or to participate in such a holistic approach to enterprise-level transformation, covering all applicable aspects in the right sequence, and building products that customers actually need rather than want by eliminating over-design and over-engineering for these solutions. Is it a similar approach for everyone? Of course not: a one-size-fits-all approach does not work for complex adaptive systems such as human organizations and especially in a digital business world, as has been described by David Snowden's Cynefin[1] framework.

Tolerated failure imprints learning better than success.

—Dave Snowden, management consultant and creator of award-winning framework for decision making

---

[1] *Harvard Business Review*, David J. Snowden and Mary E. Boone, "A Leader's Framework for Decision Making," https://hbr.org/2007/11/a-leaders-framework-for-decision-making, November 2007.

© Michael Nir 2018
M. Nir, *The Pragmatist's Guide to Corporate Lean Strategy*,
https://doi.org/10.1007/978-1-4842-3537-9_1

This framework sorts the issues facing leaders into five contexts defined by the nature of the relationship between cause and effect. Four of these—simple, complicated, complex, and chaotic—require leaders to diagnose situations and to act in contextually appropriate ways in order to lead continuous improvement opportunities, making situation-appropriate decisions at organizational level. David Snowden emphasizes the value of learning in achieving structure of an organizational change leadership and execution.

In sum, the book you are holding in your hands contains a description of a holistic approach to an organizational transformation in a flexible culture-driven and customer-centric way. This approach is complemented by ideas, best practices, anti-patterns, tools, and templates that will allow you to orchestrate and navigate the change, no matter what your role. If you bought this book, if you are investing your time in reading this chapter, this means that this book is for you.

Are all of the following practices and the overall framework applicable to your company and your situation today? No one can answer this question for you. It is up to you to explore, engage, and discover. This is a framework, not a methodology, because it defines the areas of importance, shares points of view, and offers food for thought supplemented by practical guidance. As you read through the book, you will engage **in practical exercises that will challenge you to think how these concepts apply to your specific situation.**

■ **Tip** Once you complete a section of this book and get an exercise or a question to answer, approach these assignments as a brainstorming session within your company. If you are an employee, create a Community of Practice to share ideas in a book club on the topic, experience sharing session, or on your work wiki. If you are a manager, seek opinions from your team by facilitating a team-level discussion. If you are an organization leader, consider turning part of a leadership session into a brainstorming session or a workshop on this topic and solicit opinions throughout the organization. Bring in customers as early as possible in order to validate your assumptions and co-create the value.

Use these techniques to identify your pain points and establish priorities, whether you use contemporary Post-Its or a digital board for your distributed team.[2]

---

[2]There are multiple brainstorming tools and techniques that you can use effectively for distributed teams. Some of the options include setting up a Google drawing board where all participants can type their suggestions at the same time, then group, prioritize, and discuss, resulting in agreed-upon action items. You can do this with any web conferencing software that includes whiteboarding capabilities such as Skype for Business or WebEx, or with specialized brainstorming, collaboration, and whiteboarding software such as Mural.ly, OpenBoard, or Open-Sankoré.

As you embark on this journey with me, I invite you to answer the question, which is fundamental in any coaching area, including product development and organizational coaching: What's in it for me (WiiFM)? No one except for you will be able to answer this. I am convinced this framework is a perfect fit for you and I hope that this book will provide you with food for thought, and that if you choose to pursue this change effort, it will give you highly effective practical advice and a compass to follow throughout your organizational transformation.

How? Become an Entrepreneur.

This book describes an organizational transformation journey from several perspectives. What are the steps of the journey that you need to embark on as you transform your organization? Think of it as a map that will help you navigate the transformation journey. I will start by setting the course of your transformation and its success criteria since no journey will be successful unless you know the destination The task is even more complex because your destination will change and you need to recognize these changes and adjust the course accordingly.

I describe the crew that you need to assemble on your ship in order to successfully navigate the waters. The crew has to be skilled, knowledgeable, highly collaborative, and cross-functional so that if one of them becomes unavailable, the others can carry the load.

I define the structure and the framework you will have to establish so that your ship sails steadily despite all the winds and challenges of the open ocean. Moreover, I describe the ways of continuously improving these processes and frameworks.

Finally, I define the equipment you need on board: what tools and hardware you need, how to build the knowledge to operate it, how to upgrade it on a regular and frequent basis, and most importantly, what comes next.

In sum, for each of the areas, you must define three ways of introducing and orchestrating the organizational change: people, process, and tools, described on a timeline of implementation. I will explain the product as a result of people applying tools and processes to achieve the desired result. I will also discuss the organizational ecosystem, from envisioning a new product or service initiative to implementing the minimum viable product (MVP) and further incremental delivery based on customer feedback and validated learning.

From an entrepreneurial mindset, the three sections of the book provide you with a complete map of such a journey.

Part 1: Five Lessons from Lean Startup Thinking

In this section, I discuss lean startup as a concept: how it originated, its role in organizational change, why it is revolutionary in product development, and how it is applied in today's business world. In this section, I will review five major lessons from the lean startup:

- Start with the customer in mind.
- Define and communicate the mission and vision.
- Synthesize an integrative operating model.
- Identify metrics that matter.
- Pivot or persevere.

I describe each of the concepts and their practical implementation, and review examples of how each of these concepts applies at an enterprise level. I analyze successful implementations and discuss the danger of "doing" lean agile at the enterprise vs. applying values and principles to versatile and complex business environment.

Part 2: Five Techniques to Succeed

In the second section of this book, I bring these concepts and practical steps into a single framework. I offer you a framework, not a one-size-fits-all methodology. You will have a set of tools and techniques with well-defined values and best practices while retaining the flexibility of your implementation. You will be able to present these ideas to senior management for their buy-in as a single thought-through framework and you will be able orchestrate implementation at scale while avoiding common pitfalls. This section contains multiple templates that you can use in your organization to orchestrate experimentation, reduce risk, anticipate customer needs, and predict success of your products before you start building them.

This framework covers the following topics:

- Define the mission.
- Identify customer personas.
- prototype MVP and program training
- Run experiments with customers to validate your hypotheses.
- Pivot or persevere in a build-measure-learn cycle.

What's unique about section two is that it structured around a timeline approach. I identify the emphasis of the various elements of the framework on a continuum: the first 30 days, the first 90 days, and the first 12 months. I describe them from the view point of you—the reader, the future strategist and implementer. I found that describing complex ideas using a day-in-the-life method provides simple guidelines for a successful rollout.

The goal is to enable your transformation to be a success. I provide step-by-step instructions to **ensure initial success, communicate it broadly, secure incremental funding, and establish sustainable culture change** via delegating decision-making and promoting communities of practice.

Part 3: Lessons in Building a Corporate Startup

Once you master the concepts in a simple and pragmatic way, you will start building your lean enterprise ecosystem. The goal is to achieve customer satisfaction and co-create products with them and for them. In this section, I share three mini-stories of successes and failures of enterprise lean agile transformations. There are numerous successes and multiple war stories in the journeys to agility. None of these transformations is a complete success or an absolute failure, yet some achieved their original goals while others struggled or failed.

I subtitled section 3 as "the muddy waters of reality" since in truth things never turn out as planned. With the best intentions, transformations change, impact, and are impacted by organizational realities. My objective in this section is to share the success and failure stories where best intentions meet reality and what can we learn from them.

The three mini-stories are loosely based on a plethora of engagements completed in the real world and are described from the perspectives of employees that embarked on these transformations. They describe the following goals:

- Achieve and retain leadership support.
- Consider the corporate culture.
- Evangelize across the enterprise.

While written as fiction and simplified for the purpose of this book, each of the stories shares pragmatic advice and experience from the field of a lean agile transformation, which you will be able to immediately apply to the area of your responsibility, to your company or business, and even to your family. Each journey is told through the eyes of a persona who is part of this transformation and each highlights one of the "must-haves" of a lean startup corporation. You'll learn from their experience so that you can avoid the mistakes they made and build on the successes they achieved. I discuss scaling approaches and define non-negotiables that are required to establish a cultural change.

Sustaining Your Transformation and Making It Ongoing

So what happens when a consulting organization exits a client site? This question is extremely valid. Agile coaching, for example, is viewed as a temporary endeavor until the teams move up from "shu" to "ha" to "ri" (more on this concept in Alistair Cockburn's *Agile Software Development*[3]) or from "Imitate and Assimilate" to "Transform." However, it is hard to put strict timelines on the change of values, culture, and mindset. I discuss the techniques that will allow you to make the changes "stick" after your lean startup coaches leave. The topics include

- What now? Your immediate next steps

- Why lean startup is here to stay

Within each of these topics, I suggest different ways of testing the sustainability of your lean agile implementation and I discuss non-negotiables of organizational change that allow you to feel a "bad smell" or anti-patterns, which indicate that your organization is merely following the lean agile implementation steps rather than living the values of continuous improvement, customer-centricity, and validated learning. I discuss multiple venues of sustaining this new mindset in a mature adaptive change-driven lean organization.

How Is This Information Presented?

Treat this book as a textbook. Throughout the book, I provide templates and exercises that enable you to execute on your organizational transformation goals from day one. If you would like to learn more about each specific topic, I suggest references. The only limit to the level of change you are now able to bring to your organization is defined by how open-minded you are in implementing new approaches, trying new ways of working, collaborating with your customers, motivating your teams, and delivering innovative products and services that lead to business success and employee and customer satisfaction.

Throughout the book, I use several ways of bringing your attention to the items to think about or to beware of. The conventions I use in this book are shown in Table 1-1.

---

[3]Alistair Cockburn; *Agile Software Development* (Boston, MA: Addison-Wesley Professional, 2006).

Table 1-1. Book Conventions

	Meaning
Tip	A helpful idea to help you promote and respond to the organizational change. I encourage you to use these ideas in internal workshops to promote the change in your organization. I will share specific examples of turning these ideas into action
Best Practice	The best practices are non-negotiables of your enterprise transformation. If there is anything to implement correctly, these are the concepts to follow and the steps to implement. They can be directly translated into action items for your enterprise transformation
Anti-Pattern	Beware of these common anti-patterns. If you feel that your transformation efforts go this route, pivot as soon as you can. While providing the anti-patterns, I share mitigation techniques and approaches that will allow you to get back on track.

If you have any questions along the way, feel free to contact me via my LinkedIn page or via my websites. I am excited to support you on your journey!

Five Lessons from Lean Startup Thinking

In this section, I discuss the lean startup as a concept: how it originated, its role in organizational change, why it is revolutionary in product development, and how it is applied in today's business world. In this section, I review five major lessons from the lean startup:

- Start with the customer in mind.
- Define and communicate the mission and vision.
- Synthesize an integrative operating model.
- Identify metrics that matter.
- Pivot or persevere.

I describe each of the concepts and their practical implementation, and I review examples of how each of these concepts applies at an enterprise level. I analyze successful implementations and discuss the danger of "doing" lean vs. applying values and principles to versatile and complex business environments.

As you'll see, along my journey to implement lean in the enterprise, I ran into challenges. What I read made sense; however, the actual implementation told a different story and I had to **unlearn and then relearn** some concepts to make the concepts stick.

Start with the Customer in Mind

A Persona Goes a Long Way

Jake stops at his favorite Starbucks off the Temple Place Tube station to pick up a latte, no milk, on his way to office. He works at the corporate headquarters of a large global financial institution in the city of London. Today is a big day for him because they are finally rolling out a private home loan product that has been 18 months in the making.

Jake is the business analyst, which means he was responsible for gathering the business and user requirements for the product. He spent three months creating the business requirement document (BRD), a hefty, 60-page document that detailed the specifics of the product.[1] Later he supported the program manager in overseeing development of the product features. The product was created in Bangalore, India where the bank's engineering uses an agile delivery approach. Initially Jake submitted the BRD for approval and later throughout the project he communicated the requirements to a London-based business analyst from the engineering side, who in turn communicated with the system engineer in New Delhi, India who was managing the engineering team in Bangalore.

---

[1]The BRD (business requirement document) is a document that takes months to produce and then leadership has to sign it to allow the project to proceed; however, usually nobody actually reads it…

© Michael Nir 2018
M. Nir, *The Pragmatist's Guide to Corporate Lean Strategy*,
https://doi.org/10.1007/978-1-4842-3537-9_2

When Jake entered the marble floored lobby, he saw Sarah, the program manager, and Janice, the VP of product; they looked distraught. He approached and could hear that they were speaking with a branch manager of the bank at a branch that opened early on Mondays. The new product, deployed with much fanfare, was a total blowout.

Similar feedback was received throughout the first week: the product was failing, users couldn't navigate the menus, and required functionality was either missing or broken. The bank's executives were upset, to say the least; they invested in agile project management in order to prevent these mistakes. What happened?

What I Read

Eric Ries in *The Lean Startup* describes how talking with the customer is the only way to produce successful products. That's simple enough: I should think from the perspective of the customer rather than create what I think they want. At relatively small organizations this is straightforward and can be achieved with a small kernel team.

> *You have to start with the customer experience and work backwards to the technology.*

—Steve Jobs, co-founder of Apple Inc.[2]

What Happened When I Tried Implementing in Big Corporations

Bigger organizations find it difficult to focus on the consumer.

First and foremost, they've been in business for years, they make money, and they are comfortable within the confines of the organization; they don't feel the need to interact with a consumer. Going outside of the office and actually asking a customer what they want is something they just don't do. The concept of *gemba* is foreign to them.[3] Most of them are convinced that they are not allowed to do it, that it's the job of others to interact with consumers. The same is true for developing solutions for internal consumers; the prevailing mindset is "it's not our job to ask questions."

---

[2] World Wide Developers Conference, May 1997, 52:15, http://everystevejobsvideo.com/qa-with-steve-jobs-wwdc-1997/.
[3] Japanese word for "the real place," which translates to "get out of your office; go and see; don't make assumptions; look for facts and reality in the gemba."

Inside-out thinking is a recurring challenge for enterprises. For example, traditional insurance companies focus on making it hard for the consumer to receive their money when submitting a claim. This isn't a specific hurdle but rather a mindset of the insurance company around which many of the internal processes are built. They make it hard to issue a claim, they make it difficult to get support on the status of the claim, they instill an internal mindset in which the consumer is dishonest, they follow through with slow response to consumer requests, they require paper and fax be used rather than email (blaming regulation); the list goes on and on.

Implementing outside-in thinking in these organizations is more than a well-designed exercise in creating a persona. Rather, it is an ongoing battle to break free from the prevailing mindset of "the consumer is our enemy" and "there's a zero sum game between us and the consumer" to embracing collaboration with the consumer. The only way to truly embrace "start with the customer in mind" is through the construction of a concrete persona. Having executives participate in sessions with *real people* as part of structuring the persona has a tremendous impact and leads to true empathy; the outside-in thinking usually follows.

Anti-Pattern In many cases, there is an assumption that people who create software know what their customers actually need. There are two problems with that: the first is assuming that there is a single homogenous customer type. There never is. There are multiple customers with conflicting demands and preferences, so it is important to identify their types and make decisions about who your customers actually are. Second, you can't know what the customers need until you talk to them and ideally give them a prototype to try out and provide feedback on. Fall in love with the problem, not a solution. It is only through empathy and trial and failure that you can get practical feedback from your customer, not by imposing the proposed solutions and hoping that they will resonate with the customers.

Summarizing what I've experienced and heard in bigger organizations when I presented the concept of focusing on the customer:

- They've been operating for years with the same approach, and most likely this is an inside-out view of the market, which is contrary to embracing a consumer-centric point of view.

- They merely develop products for external consumers. Other people gather requirements for these products, so when they get it wrong, it's their fault!

- They develop products for internal users that are less "fancy" and don't require all the "fluff" of customer focus.

- They are not a startup.
- They are not Apple.

It is true that bigger global organizations find it more challenging to embrace this concept of focusing on the customer since they have existing frameworks in place as well as regulations and stipulations that stand in the way of delivering what customers need; and it is true that they are not startups and that not all organizations can be Apple. BUT, in today's competitive environment, they have no alternative; they must align to the customer or perish.

Think John Deere

When I hear big corporates tell us that they can't focus on the customer in the true sense, I am reminded of a conversation with a German petrochemical engineering and manufacturing conglomerate in Manheim. I received a call from a senior manager in product development; it was the same company that I delivered lean workshops to years before. He asked for help with a lean transformation and implementing a consumer engagement model, since the company was struggling with both. I asked, "You're a company with 150 years of corporate baggage, why do you want to undergo this transformation?" He replied, "We don't. We really and truly don't, but we have no choice because John Deere is kicking us to the curb."

John Deere as a lean transformation role model might surprise you because as it is a corporation headquartered in Blackrock, Illinois, not a fancy Silicon Valley technological giant. John Deere embraced lean agile thinking in development. In an interview, the John Deere Scaled Agile transformation leader shared that there is never a good time for significant change, and sometimes it seems easier to continue to do what you have always been doing. But the world is changing rapidly, and the customers and market demands that the company change too.

What I Learned as I Adapted the Concept in a Corporation

Remember the example of the bank?

When I analyzed the failure of the product with Jake, Sarah, Janice and the executive leadership, I sensed their aversion to startup terminology, so we had to dress the concept of starting with the customer in mind in a way that was less threatening and more in line with their thinking.

We discussed the business requirement journey: the number of handoffs that a requirement makes between the customer and the engineering team. Actually, while a requirement was referred to as a "requirement" on the business side, it was termed "user story" by the agile development team. By the time the team was working on the user story, it had been handed off four times, translated from English to dev-speak and some Hindi, so it lost most of the context.

The development team in Bangalore, true to agile practices, participated in backlog grooming[4] with the System Analyst in New Delhi and occasionally with the Business Analyst from the IT side in London; however, they were twice removed from the internal customer of the system, the user at the bank. At no time during the 18-month project did the development team get a chance to receive feedback from the user; it was always through proxies.

No wonder the product failed.

What I Implemented

We were constrained by the distributed team, the language barriers, and practices that the bank had in place that made it difficult to focus on the customer.

I asked product leadership the following questions:

- How do we minimize the mileage of the requirement journey?
- What is the minimal team interaction that is required to gain a better understanding of the requirement?
- Who should be a part of the team?
- What format should we use to communicate our requirement discussions?
- What are the agreed definitions for requirements, user stories, capabilities, features, epics, etc.?

I offered two corporate adaptations to starting with the customer in mind:

- Focus on the most impactful horizontal interaction between the people who develop the product and those who will be using it, and enable communications on a weekly basis.
- Create, refine, and relate to a persona.

---

[4]Backlog grooming is an agile approach to creating and refining the user stories, an ongoing activity involving the product owner and team to develop the product backlog so that the top items are ready for delivery by the team.

The first was based on observations we had concerning collaboration with users and customers at big organizations. Collaboration often occurs at the initiation and completion of a big project, involves a large group of people, and doesn't allow time for emphasizing with the user or customer. The Bangalore team might have interacted with users once at the beginning of the project, but this interaction was limited in scope, controlled top down by the business analyst, and wasn't a two-way conversation.

Instead we suggested that the team engage in discussions as the product was being built between users, marketing, sales, engineers, operations, and others based on the need. The meetings were framed as a discovery process; the team was encouraged to be curious about the users' experiences and environment.

The second adaptation was using a lightweight persona as a method to develop understanding. Persona development is an increasingly popular and effective tool in designing web interfaces and is espoused by design thinking and more recently Lean UX. Personas are constructs produced by analyzing and aggregating the characteristics of users and building them into profiles of typical users. The traditional versions take a lot of research and time to put together and analyze in a scientific and meaningful context. More often than not the tool tends to be limited to user experience experts and product managers.

The team adapted the practice to include a wider audience both in discussing and structuring the persona, and later on referring to the persona when making important decisions concerning the functionality of the product.

The team created a persona they called *Tim the banker*. Notice that by merely identifying gender and name they limited the problem and solution options. Actually, by giving a persona a name the team uncovered many assumptions about the behavior, experience, and aptitude of the user.[5] The persona in itself provides opportunities for assumption validation, which I discuss later in the book.

Among other benefits in using a persona rather than quoting demographics is the increased level of intimacy the team develops with the user. The team brainstormed various aspects of Tim's work and social experiences. They focused on his day at the bank, what is he trying to achieve, what is challenging him, and what tasks he needs to get done.

When Jake, Sarah, and Janice prepared for the next project, they had a framework to start with the customer in mind and they kept the persona center stage while the agile development team created the product.

---

[5]Big Think, Sam McNerney, "Drunk Tank Pink: A Q&A with Adam Alter," http://bigthink. com/insights-of-genius/drunk-tank-pink-a-qa-with-adam-alter, March 21, 2013.

Key Learning: Starting with the customer in mind is crucial in aligning what we develop to what people need and removing feature waste. While straightforward in smaller organizations, it can be adapted to corporations by tweaking it in such a way that the team has direct contact with their customers throughout envisioning, development, and further product enhancements.

■ **Tip** When creating personas to represent customer types, there are several non-negotiables the teams need to keep in mind:

1. Personas need to be well described. In the bank example below, creating a "customer" persona would not be helpful. It is important to collect as many details about Tim as possible: how tech savvy Tim is, what drives his behavior, what computer system he uses, if he prefers a mobile phone to a laptop. What are his drivers: Ease of use? Reliability? Time? Is he a decision-maker in major areas? If not, who is? Then I would create a manager persona, an auditor, and so forth.

2. Personas need to be very specific. There is no generic customer. There is Max the Millennial who invested in several successful startups. Max has his platinum account with the bank. Max uses mobile devices and keeps all his data in the cloud. Max does not care about graphics as long as he can access data easily and quickly. He also wants the app to be modern and sleek and provide maximum functionality for using digital payment media. There is also Ted, a retired accountant who accesses the application from a desktop in his apartment. His vision is not as good anymore so he is looking for accessibility features. He hates new graphics because it disrupts his user experience and does not like when new features are introduced because it requires adjustment. Max and Ted require different user experiences and some of their expectations are contradictory, so it is important to identify the actual customer.

3. Go out of the building and research who the customer actually is and whether they have the need you are trying to address. In many cases, we assume personas and their needs without actually talking to them. As an example, a test prep company saw students as their primary customers. They went out of their way to tailor their product to the needs of multiple user types: a fresh high school graduate, someone with a work experience, a graduate student, a law student, a medical student, etc. When they went out of the building and started asking how the decisions were made, they found out that for several of these categories, it was not the students who were decision makers, it was parents. So, while both categories cared about proven results, students cared about sophisticated interface and well-designed test practice, and the parents cared about functionality that would allow them to view the progress of their kids and how much time they spent using the software. And in case of high school students, there are parents who make purchasing decisions related to their kids' test prep course. The only way to find this out is to go out and actually speak with both groups.

In essence, whether you are starting a new project or are attempting to enhance an existing one, start by identifying the right customers and developing customer personas. And once you do, refine the personas continuously as you learn more and more about your customers. Place persona pictures and descriptions of their "journeys" as "information radiators" around your office and on your intranet and let your employees empathize with them and their stories. This will take your product to the next level and increase employee motivation at the same time. Note that persona descriptions are specific to the needs of your business.

Besides being a useful product-building exercise, persona creation is a way to align the organization with who the stakeholders see as the primary users and what the interests of this person are. I recommend a two-step exercise, which can be done at executive level as well as within the delivery organization. Step one is to identify your personas and create "persona cards" and then share and align on a single vision as a team or the company. Step two is to go out of the building to validate your assumptions about these personas based on your analytics and call center experience; reach out to these users, individual customers, and institutions, and reconcile your assumptions with reality. The results are frequently eye opening.

Tip Review the description of Max the Millennial depicted in the section below. All persona descriptions are business-specific. What business do you think the company is in that created this persona?

SAMPLE PERSONA: MAX THE MILLENNIAL

Max the Millennial

Max the Millennial is **tech savvy** and **socially aware**. He cares about doing the right things for society while being thoughtful in his investments. He performs basic banking functions through digital channels. He needs up-to-date information and does not care much about personable customer service because he is doing all transactions via his Mac or his iPhone app. He cares about application performance and sleek app design as well as all modern payment media.

In his 20s, Max uses mobile devices and keeps all his data in the cloud. Max does not care about website graphics as long as he can access data easily and quickly. He also wants the app to be modern and sleek and provide maximum functionality for using digital payment media of all sorts. In the last two years, **he never visited a bank in person**—no need, since he values his time and the convenience of digital transactions.

Max lives in a rural area in close proximity to a large city so he is in the market for a new car (he prefers leasing one). He does not take risks but is open to experiments in his investments and spending. His loyalty is to people, not institutions, so if another bank offers better services, charity contribution opportunities, or has a reputation of being socially responsible, he will gladly switch, as long as the process does not require a time investment on his part.

Three words to describe Max: **financially solid, tech-savvy, traveler**.

Name: Max

Age: 27

Lives: NJ

Education: M.S.

Occupation: Programmer

Anti-Pattern In many organizations, personas are treated as a sign of being "modern:" pictures are laminated on the wall and persona stories are included in employee booklets. Personas are as living and breathing as the people who they represent. Avoid creating static types of your users and customers; think of them as continuously evolving as the customer persona evolves along with a company's understanding of the target audience and their needs.

Define and Communicate the Mission and Vision

Align the Transformation

"Would you tell me, please, which way I ought to go from here?"

"That depends a good deal on where you want to get to," said the Cat.

"I don't much care where—" said Alice.

"Then it doesn't matter which way you go," said the Cat.

"—so long as I get SOMEWHERE," Alice added as an explanation.

"Oh, you're sure to do that," said the Cat, "if you only walk long enough."

—Lewis Carroll, *Alice's Adventures in Wonderland* (1865)

© Michael Nir 2018
M. Nir, *The Pragmatist's Guide to Corporate Lean Strategy*,
https://doi.org/10.1007/978-1-4842-3537-9_3

In 1814, Ivan Krylov, Russia's best-known fabulist and probably the most epigrammatic of all Russian authors, wrote a fable called "Swan, Pike, and Crawfish" (translated by Sergey Armeyskov[1]):

> When partners can't agree
>
> Their dealings come to naught
>
> And trouble is their labor's only fruit.
>
> Once Crawfish, Swan, and Pike
>
> Set out to pull a loaded cart,
>
> And all together settled in the traces;
>
> They pulled with all their might, but still the cart refused to budge!
>
> The load it seemed was not too much for them:
>
> Yet Crawfish scrambled backwards,
>
> Swan strained up skywards, Pike pulled toward the sea.
>
> Who's guilty here and who is right is not for us to say —
>
> But anyway **the cart's still there today**.

The last line, "the cart's still there today," became a proverb which means "nothing has changed" as attributed to situations where there is a lot of effort and no alignment. This is exactly why the power of shared objectives is so important.

As you can see from the two examples above, it is important to

1. Have compelling, timely, well communicated objectives (which has been well defined by the mnemonic SMART, which stands for Specific, Measurable, Achievable, Relevant, and Time-bound).

2. Have these objectives aligned, agreed upon, and continuously measured across the organization in a cascading way both top-down and bottom-up. The concept that I find most successful in a corporate environment is OKRs (objectives and key results.)

---

[1] Russianuniverse, Sergey Armeyskov, "Ivan Krylov's Fable 'Swan, Pike & Crawfish,' " https://russianuniverse.org/2014/04/06/ivan-krylovs-fable-swan-pike-and-crawfish/, 2014.

What I Read

While the objectives need to be specific, this is not the starting point. In order for the objectives to be aligned on, it is important to start with a vision, develop a strategy to align on this vision, and only then move to implementation. In his eight-stage process, John Kotter sees two steps (One: developing a vision and strategy, and two: communicating the change vision[2]) following immediately the creation of the sense of urgency and creating the guiding coalition. Once the cause is established and the leadership team is formed, the next step is to align on a compelling mission and vision. This is why mission statements are so important for future success.

The mission statement is a cross-company effort created by leadership at all levels. It has been noticed time and again that if the mission statement is not compelling enough, then business success is not possible. For example, if the mission is purely revenue-based, it is not sufficient for employees to be intrinsically motivated to go above and beyond to achieve it. If, however, the mission appeals to their sense of purpose, they will produce outstanding outcomes and money will come as a result, and even if not, they will not be discouraged and will pivot because the goal will still be important to them. In cases of financial motivation, the first failure discourages the team and prevents future pivots in implementing the vision.

■ **Anti-Pattern** Mission statements have to be both compelling and realistic. Having a compelling mission statement that is not supported by a company's values or is just simply not achievable (at least in the visible time frame) creates the opposite effect.

What I Learned from Implementing These Concepts in Big Corporations

Senior executives are convinced that the vision they crafted is shared by the entire organization. This is not in alignment with reality; my experience has shown that in many organizations the opposite is often true. While the vision is shared among senior leadership, employees are not contributing to the vision, and while it may seem that communication channels are open, they are not. When asked, employees can't articulate the vision and moreover can't relate and connect the vision to their daily activities.

---

[2]John Kotter, *Leading Change Part II:The Eight-Stage Process,* (Brighton, MA: Harvard Business Review Press, 2012).

Consider the insurance company that started on the path of lean startup and put forth a vision of a complete lean agile transformation. When middle management had to articulate requirements for a new policy administration system, they reverted to recreating the system already in place: a legacy system that was slow, often requiring manual processes, and in no way supported the transformational vision. Later in this chapter I share the concept of an agile open space to create, refine, and communicate a vision among many participants; I learned the hard way that vision sessions that occur in an offsite and include a small group of senior stakeholders rarely succeed.

To discuss the experience, the logical first step is to review some examples of leading companies. Let's play a game: guess the companies behind the following vision statements:

- "We believe that we are on the face of the earth to make great products and that's not changing. We are constantly focusing on innovating. We believe in the simple, not the complex. We believe that we need to own and control the primary technologies behind the products that we make, and participate only in markets where we can make a significant contribution. We believe in saying no to thousands of projects, so that we can really focus on the few that are truly important and meaningful to us. We believe in deep collaboration and cross-pollination of our groups, which allow us to innovate in a way that others cannot. And frankly, we don't settle for anything less than excellence in every group in the company, and we have the self-honesty to admit when we're wrong and the courage to change." [3]

- "Our mission is to establish <company> as the premier purveyor of the finest coffee in the world while maintaining our uncompromising principles while we grow."[4]

- "Our mission is to help our consumers thrive in a sustainable economy where people, profit, and planet are in balance."[5]

---

[3]Panmore Institute, Christine Rowland, "Apple's Vision Statement & Mission Statement," http://panmore.com/apple-mission-statement-vision-statement, January 29, 2017.
[4]Panmore Institute, Gregory Lawrence, "Starbucks Coffee's Vision Statement & Mission Statement," http://panmore.com/starbucks-coffee-vision-statement-mission-statement, January 29, 2017.
[5]Panmore Institute, Nathaniel Smithson, "Nike, Inc. Vision Statement & Mission Statement," http://panmore.com/nike-inc-vision-statement-mission-statement, February 7, 2017.

- "To be Earth's most customer-centric company, where customers can find and discover anything they might want to buy online."[6]
- "To help people stay connected with friends and family, to discover what's going on in the world, and to share and express what matters to them."[7]

Here's another example: "The Group's goal is to offer attractive, safe, and environmentally sound vehicles which can compete in an increasingly tough market and set world standards in their respective class." This is the Volkswagen Group's mission statement from 2013,[8] before the story broke in 2015 that Volkswagen deliberately buried emissions results in its software. With no mission or shared values, there is no hope for achieving these goals ethically and business-wide.

I had worked for an educational company that had a mission of becoming the best educator in the world. This happened when online education was blossoming, when new remote education and "teaching from the back of the classroom" techniques were becoming more and more popular. There was a strive for education to become more affordable using online sources: coursera.com was already becoming a mainstream company, and yet this company was ignoring the signs of a changing world and continuing to prioritize its traditional tutoring practices while attempting to use modern technology to sustain old business models. So in big town-halls when company executives were presenting their mission of "being the world leader in education," you could look around the room and see that it did not resonate with the audience. In fact, it produced the opposite effect, demonstrating that senior leadership was out of touch with reality.

It took this group of leaders a while to realize the misalignment and, to their credit, they changed the mission statement to a more compelling and more realistic one of "to help every student realize their potential and achieve their educational and career goals." This brings up an important point regarding mission statements that are internally facing (I do not believe that the town hall version was shared broadly) vs. mission statements that are aimed at creating a positive image of the company and promoting its brand. Ideally, a mission statement should be the same for employees and the public, which is the case if the mission and vision are authentic, ethical, and realistic.

[6]Panmore Institute, Gregory Lawrence; "Amazon.com Inc.'s Vision Statement & Mission Statement," http://panmore.com/amazon-com-inc-vision-statement-mission-statement-analysis, February 12, 2017.
[7]Panmore Institute, Nathaniel Smithson, "Facebook Inc.'s Vision Statement & Mission Statement," http://panmore.com/facebook-inc-vision-statement-mission-statement, February 7, 2017.
[8]Strategic Management Insight, Ovidijus Jurevicius, "Mission statement of Volkswagen," www.strategicmanagementinsight.com/mission-statements/volkswagen-mission-statement.html, September 14, 2013.

Communicate your mission statement and seek feedback on each and every aspect of it. Based on personas identified previously, identify your audience and look at your statement through their eyes. To do so, do internal brainstorming, reach out to your customers, and avoid letting your internal marketing organization define your company's DNA without direct feedback from the people you work for. Have your employees do brainstorming, debates, have competitions for best wording, polls for most compelling statement; in other words, crowdsource your vision and mission statement. Stay authentic but also let it be a little bit of a future vision and a little bit of a status quo that reflects your ongoing values. And once you come up with it, communicate it in information radiators, conversations, awards: "make it stick." You can find great advice on how to make it stick in a book by brothers Heath called *Made to Stick: Why Some Ideas Survive and Others Die.*[9]

In *Made to Stick*, the authors use the mnemonic SUCCES to share the constituents of a compelling statement:

- Simple
- Unexpected
- Concrete
- Credible
- Emotional
- Stories

The same concept applies to the mission and vision statements.

In their book *Switch*,[10] the same Dan and Chip Heath suggest a helpful technique called "destination postcards" which provide an inspirational and vivid picture from the near-term future. By pointing to an attractive destination, the visionary applies his strengths to figure out how to get there, instead of getting lost in analysis.

---

[9]Chip Heath and Dan Heath, *Made to Stick: Why Some Ideas Survive and Others Die* (New York, NY: Random House, 2007).
[10]Chip Heath and Dan Heath, *Switch: How to Change Things When Change Is Hard,* (New York, NY: Crown Business, 2010).

■ **Best Practice**   Many town hall gatherings that I witnessed are top-down directives, where senior leadership communicates the vision and mission with the employees. I experimented with an alternative approach whereby 250 employees collaborate with senior leadership to develop and clarify a vision. I employed an Agile Open Space approach[11] to engage the big team and a polling tool such as PollEverywhere to summarize discussion and rank options. Figure 3-1 demonstrates a planning event. I found that utilizing this collaborative planning approach for big audiences increases the buy-in of the vision and the OKRs.

Figure 3-1. Agile Open Space with big room planning of vision

---

[11]Agile Open Space is an approach to involve usually large number of participants in an open-ended discussion using state-of-the-art facilitation best practices.

What I Learned from Implementing OKRs at Large Companies

The most important part of progressing from the high-level mission and vision statement is to create goals and objectives that are measurable and solve an existing problem (compare with John Kotter's "sense of urgency"). In *The Lean Startup*, Eric Ries shares that he always pushes his team to first answer four questions before building a new product:

1. Do consumers recognize that they have the problem you are trying to solve?

2. If there was a solution, would they buy it?

3. Would they buy it from us?

4. Can we build a solution for that problem?"[12]

These are fundamental questions to answer before starting any new product development; they provide a practical way to validate your vision. If the answer to any of them is negative, there is no reason to create this solution. This sequence is also extremely important because you need to understand what customers need before proposing a solution. The principle is "fall in love with the problem, not with your solution." Active listening is as key here as it is in personal relationships, just in a different form.

And finally, once the company listens and understands the customer needs well enough, there are several key techniques that help align at an enterprise level. The one I am going to discuss here is OKRs (objectives and key results). It's not a new concept; it was first used by Intel and then implemented by Google and successfully used by many startups. See a "non-fictional fiction" called *Radical Focus* by Christina Wodtke.[13]

OKRs are now becoming a successful means of aligning objectives and key results across major enterprises, top-down and bottom-up. A cascading way of aligning on common objectives and measuring progress on a continuous basis across the organization changes the way how progress is achieved, measured, and rewarded in a corporate setting. By providing well-aligned OKRS, an organization creates a roadmap that aligns with its long-term vision and mission. This brings vision, ideation, and execution together at an enterprise level.

---

[12]Eric Ries, *The Lean Startup: How today's entrepreneurs use continuous innovation to create radically successful businesses* (New York, NY: Crown Business, 2011).

[13]Christina Wodtke, *Radical Focus: Achieving Your Most Important Goals with Objectives and Key Results* (Cucina Media, 2016), https://www.amazon.com/Radical-Focus-Achieving-Important-Objectives/dp/0996006028/ref=sr_1_1?ie=UTF8&qid=1521675760&sr=8-1&keywords=christina+wodtke.

OKRs as shorter-term objectives need to align to the "destination postcard" (success criteria described by Dan and Chip Heath in *Switch* and mentioned above) and needs to be measured; otherwise the goal will be never achieved.

There are multiple ways of grading OKRs to define whether the result has been achieved, but the major concept is that OKRs should never be used for performance assessment purposes. They need to be aspirational but realistic, and created by people who want to achieve them in accordance with the cascading enterprise objectives.

■ **Anti-Pattern** OKRs are different from KPIs or from the management by objective (MBO) approach because they specifically should not be aligned to performance reviews. Otherwise, employees will choose safe OKRs rather than aspirational ones. In addition, OKRs should be created by employees in sync with company objectives, openly discussed, and broadly communicated, rather than imposed top-down. In a 175-year old data company, there was a manager who was continuously rewriting the OKRs that one of his team members came up with. When the team member objected to this action, feeling that the changes were unrealistic and irrelevant, this manager told the leader of the team that they must meet their OKRs or he would fire the leader and the rest of the team. No wonder the members of this team left the company one by one, followed by their leader. In this case, OKRs hurt the company rather than promoted a shared vision.

For example, if a public educational company wishes to provide winning test prep strategies for students, the organization has a responsibility to its shareholders to increase profit per share as well as to the students and their parents to enable them achieve high text results. Within the organization, there are tutors who need to teach students to improve their test scores; marketing to make students, parents, and their schools aware of the opportunities; sales to provide helpful pricing strategies and execute sales; and facilities to provide classrooms or technology to develop and support learning apps. Each of these functions supports the corporate goal from its own perspective.

OKRs have to be measurable and specific. From a business perspective, it could be 3% growth per share during a calendar year. From a student perspective, it could be 5% higher average test score. The Google way of grading OKRs is widely accepted (0 to 1, where 0 means "have not started" and 1 means "fully achieved"). From this perspective, 1 is as bad as 0 because it means that the OKR was not ambitious, while somewhere around 0.7 is considered a success. In my experience, I've seen OKRs measured in percentages as well as on a specific scale, such as Net Promoter Score of 0 to 10.

Bain's Net Promoter System is based on the fundamental perspective that every company's customers can be divided into three categories. "Promoters" are loyal enthusiasts who keep buying from a company and urge their friends to do the same. "Passives" are satisfied but unenthusiastic customers who can be easily wooed by the competition. And "detractors" are unhappy customers trapped in a bad relationship. Customers can be categorized based on their answer to the ultimate question: "How likely are you to recommend our company to a friend or colleague?" It's a 0-10 scale with 10 being extremely likely to recommend and 0 being not at all likely. Responses to this question are divided into three categories: promoters (rating of 9-10), passives (rating of 7-8), and detractors (rating of 0-6). This scale is sometimes used as a metric for OKR grading or as an OKR measurement in a consumer-facing businesses.

Whichever measurement it is, the OKRs should be pregraded to remove ambiguity. Pregrading happens when OKRs are created, discussed, and agreed upon in a group setting where the group agrees what is 0.3, 0.5, 0.7, and 1. For example, if an OKR is to increase average student SAT scores by 20%, they may agree that any increase would give them 0.3, 10% increase is 0.5, 15% increase is 0.7, and 20% increase is 1, and then everything in between will become intuitive. This pregrading takes any ambiguity out of the final discussion of "Did we meet our OKRs or not?" For this reason, binary OKRs are rarely a good idea because they may be extremely demotivating. For example, if there is an OKR to get a Webby award for the best learning app, and the award goes to another company, is it a 0? What if this app got a "customer appreciation" award or a Codie award? Is submission for nomination a considered progress merely because it brings required learning for the next year? All of these questions can be avoided if this OKR is not formulated as "yes/no."

The cadence is another frequent topic as related to OKRs. OKRs are supposed to be of a shorter term than company objectives and the frequency depends on the nature and size of the business. For corporates, a proved duration is an annual OKR setting process with quarterly objectives and alignment every quarter including grading with an opportunity to pivot quarterly or more frequently. Given that OKRs are still high-level objectives, there is normally a limited need to pivot within a quarter; however, in highly disruptive business areas this is not uncommon. Felipe Castro advises on the following cadence:

- Annual strategic OKRs for the company (and sometimes for very large departments and business units)

- Quarterly tactical OKRs for the teams, with a mid-quarter review

The number of OKRs reflects the company's ability to prioritize its objectives. The key is relentless prioritization. In the example of the manager who tied OKRs to individual performance, the same manager insisted on each of his teams having a set of OKRs and then added his own on top, thus creating 10 or more OKRs for a 20-person organization. This was unmanageable and created unbalanced workloads for employees. The lesson is that the number should be 3-5 (and no more) for each team.

Finally, let's touch on the concept of ownership, the most controversial topic within the OKR concept. Should there be individual OKRs, which create potential conflicts between functions and individuals, or team-based OKRs only (such as Sales OKRs, Marketing OKRs, etc.)? My suggested approach is to make OKRs team-specific rather than putting a name on OKRs so that they do not become a threatening management tool for those managers who exhibit top-down thinking. I've heard concerns that team ownership means no ownership without a name attached to each OKR and people won't take responsibility if they do not feel personally accountable. **I believe that this approach comes from a lack of trust and misinterpretation of the concept of a "team" in a modern work environment.** In a healthy environment, people feel accountability and association with their team strongly enough and they do not fear individual responsibility to motivate them to achieve their goals.

▦ Best Practice

1. Answer the following questions:

- What is your organizational vision?
- What is your group's vision?
- How is it communicated and aligned with the broader organization?
- Is it posted on the walls?
- How frequently do you share it and measure progress?
- How excited are people to share the objectives?

2. Ask/poll people in your organization. Are your answers and theirs in sync?

3. Ideate a list of action items to communicate, align, and inspire your team and your organization via internal social media, town halls, training, and/or lunch & learn. Be as creative as possible within your organization's culture and beyond.

Synthesize an Integrative Operating Model

Lean Startup: Agile, Scaled Agile, Lean UX, and Design Thinking

Jake, the business analyst who creates business requirement documents (BRD); Sarah, the program manager; Janice, the VP of product who is responsible for managing and delivering projects and products; and others at the bank headquarters are familiar with *The Lean Startup*. They read it and acknowledged the merits; practically, though, they saw little use for it in their own work, however compelling the concept. In their mind, the agile delivery framework that's in place coupled with the innovation lab that implements Lean UX to learn and create consumer experiences are the manifestations of lean startup.

In another part of the world, the development team in India is using the scrum method, an agile delivery framework, to collaborate and complete the user stories (a.k.a. requirements) appearing in Jake's BRD. The team has a Scrum

© Michael Nir 2018
M. Nir, *The Pragmatist's Guide to Corporate Lean Strategy*,
https://doi.org/10.1007/978-1-4842-3537-9_4

Master who is similar to a project manager in some sense and yet different in the way she interacts with the team and motivates the team to improve. The system engineer in New Delhi, India is also the product owner for the team; he translates the BRD that Jake provided into a backlog of user stories.

The development team sees little of the London-based innovation efforts. Occasionally they interact with the Lean UX innovation lab team and an external lean consultant from Boston, creating features and functionalities from disparate assumption validation exercises.

However, these segregated efforts are not part of the bigger development effort on which the product delivery organization is focused.

In this process-filled environment, leadership assumed that they were covered, so to speak, and that the features and products developed would be consumer-delighting MVPs. They were not expecting the colossal failure that emerged from Jake, Sarah, and Janice's efforts.

What I Read

Lean startup as defined and described by Steve Blank[1] and Eric Ries[2] is the foundation of what I refer to as business agility. *The Startup Way* provides the engine for the process of ongoing experimentation, validation of business hypotheses with customers, and using the validated learning to decide whether the next step is to pivot (try other products, solutions, target markets, etc.; there may be multiple types of pivots based on customer feedback) or persevere in the business they would like to pursue. This is a brilliant concept. However, success in each individual case depends on how thoughtfully it is implemented: whether the right experiment is performed to validate the most foundational hypothesis, whether the right customers were identified and the number of the customers was "just right" (not too many, not too few), whether the right questions were asked and the right conclusions were made based on aggregated answers. This is a combination of data science and business intuition, market knowledge and active listening. In sum, it's an art and a science at the same time. Lean startup is the glue that holds all this reasoning, analysis, and customer experience together.

[1]Steve Blank, The Four Steps to the Epiphany, 2nd Ed. (K&S Ranch, 2013).
[2]Eric Ries, *The Lean Startup: How Today's Entrepreneurs use continuous innovation to create radically successful businesses* (New York, NY: Crown Business, 2011); Eric Ries, *The Startup Way. How Modern Companies Use Entrepreneurial Management to Transform Culture and Drive Long-Term Growth* (New York, NY: Currency, 2017).

As an actual example from my experience, we called 100 random people on the phone (identified by Amazon Mechanical Turk) and asked them if they would be interested in a new super-efficient weight-loss pill. Over 80% responded that they would like to try it. When the pill was produced and launched into the market at a relatively low cost compared with competition, sales were less than 1% of prediction. Why? The answer is easy: **"would you like to try"** questions are theoretical and do not require commitment. Thus, if you ask a question whether someone would like to try a product or service, especially the one that makes them more physically attractive or socially accepted, who would say no? Besides, the questions were asked to MTurks who took a low-paid job to make an extra dollar on a research call like this one; this is probably not the right audience because it is unlikely that MTurks would have money to invest in purchasing a new weight-loss pill and even if they do, there is tough competition on the market for low-priced weight-loss products. All of this invalidates the experiment and makes its results misleading.

In a big data company I worked with, one of the lean startup teams wanted to validate the assumption that "small businesses want to grow." You do not need lean startup coaches to understand that this is a wrong assumption because most likely every small business would want to grow. What needs to be validated are their pain points and barriers for growth. Do they have trouble finding customers and suppliers? What specifically is the problem with the suppliers? Are the prices too high? Is reliability an issue? Distance? Quality of their products? And in each case, you need to be specific to the industry, business type, customer types, possibly geography, demographics, and so on.

Have you recently tried to buy a paper atlas in a bookstore? A few years ago you would have prefered a GPS to a paper map. Today, smartphones have replaced GPSs with their navigation functionality providing more convenience at a fraction of the cost. Does it mean that the business is disrupting itself over and over again? What does it mean for large, well-established enterprises? What is the right way for established businesses to use technological advancements to their advantage and integrate innovation into business success?

Lean startup is a popular concept because it provides a way for large, established enterprises to survive disruption in a modern, fast-paced world. Lean Enterprise, Lean UX, and agile delivery are popular frameworks that need to be demystified and translated into action. To understand how to use "the lean way" concept, it helps to analyze the roots and the constituents, which are the following:

- Lean brings in the concept of value creation and elimination of waste as well as personal accountability for the outcome.

- Agile brings in the concept of team-based (no longer individual) iterative delivery of value to the customer while staying customer-centric. However, most implementations

I've witnessed tended to silo agile to product development and engineering in particular. The relationship between lean and agile is complex. Some agilists do not even see a direct relationship. Even those who recognize that the agile mindset is based on lean principles of value delivery, reduction of waste, and system thinking frequently have a perception that while lean is a manufacturing approach that focuses on minimizing costs by eliminating waste and improving process efficiencies, agile is just the application of the lean mindset to software delivery with a set of processes around it. This is only partially accurate because agile, and specifically Scrum, bring two important concepts into lean: incremental delivery and cross-functional team-based execution.

- Scaled agile aligns values across the enterprise and introduces multiple value chains, thus eliminating cross-team conflicts of interest and unmanaged dependencies governed by relentless prioritization based on value delivery and organizational objectives.

- Design thinking and Lean UX[3] bring in customer-centricity and a concept of minimum viable product into delivery cadence.

- Lean startup (or "the startup way") combine these concepts by creating a cohesive framework of experimentation based on validated learning (a new implementation of the lean build-measure-learn loop) while using metrics to drive decisions.

According to Version One's *The 2016 State of Agile Report*, common corporate challenges include slow product delivery, inability to manage changing priorities, challenges with delivery predictability and visibility, all closely coupled with low employee morale and multiple difficulties related to managing a distributed workforce across cultures and continents. I experienced similar challenges at the companies I worked for, which affected our ability to quickly deliver products that delighted our customers and thus impeded business success. Examples included migrating customers to new platforms, onboarding third-party vendors, consolidating sales assets globally, and renewing service contracts with customers; in each case, we identified a need to simplify, automate, and streamline the process and make it delightful and productive for our customers, internal and external.

---

[3]Jeff Gothelf and Josh Seiden, *Lean UX: Applying Lean Principles to Improve User Experience* (Sebastopol, California: O'Reilly Media, 2013).

What Happened When I Tried Implementing in Big Corporations

The organizations I helped to create a lean startup engine already had a myriad of frameworks in place. Many were using agile as a delivery method, on top of which they implemented a scaled agile delivery to manage multiple delivery teams. In an internal system transformation at a Fortune 100 insurance company, they called their scaled agile delivery mechanism "the factory" and each delivery team used scrum to manage itself. At the same enterprise, they had UX experts and a Lean UX delivery team that had its own development resources. In addition, there was an ongoing DEVOPS effort to enable faster delivery of results across operations.

This familiar landscape exemplifies the well-known silos that impede the benefits that supposedly emerge from the various frameworks. I experienced agile and Lean UX initiatives that impacted parts of the organization without improving overall business outcomes. I knew that we had to take a different approach when creating a lean startup engine; otherwise it would become another failed improvement effort. The challenge we had, though, was that lean startup discusses a vision of entrepreneurship but fails to provide a guiding framework of how to get there.

Best Pratice   There are common mistakes with Lean Pilots (Eric Ries has a similar concept called a "Golden Sword"). First, clear expectation-setting is very important. Since the roles of Product Owner, Scrum Master, and being a member of a cross-functional team were new to the Pilot crews, we needed to have clear descriptions of what was expected, the time they should allocate to the initiative, and the ownership they would take. There were regular team "stand-up meetings" (the term comes from Scrum) where everyone was expected to participate; the absence of a team member slowed down the whole team. Team members owned results as part of their team, participated in team demos (a showcase of their work every iteration), and held retrospectives (regular continuous improvement sessions).

The second frequent mistake is overworking team members who do these pilots on top of their daily jobs. The team member's managers must agree to a predefined time allocation and restructure their current deliverables so that this responsibility doesn't come on top of the person's existing job, thus creating unsustainable pace for the team member. We set a clear expectation from the outset of who should do what and of how much time to allocate to each of the projects—and of course, anyone could say "no". It was our responsibility to create a safe space where everyone had a choice to join a Pilot crew or not.

We also learned that people really love working as part of a cross-functional and cross-level team. Once I asked one of our corporate lawyers who had just gotten involved with one of the teams whether she enjoyed working with other people and about her experience as a Product Owner on a Lean Pilot. She said, "I have always worked in the same way, mostly on my own, but working in a team has turned my world upside down. It shows me I am part of something bigger." That was a big eye-opener.

It's also important to recognize the value of combining lean, lean startup, and agile as a way to enjoy the "best of three worlds" and to create a system in which rapid validation provides a better chance to solve company-wide problems.

Finally, never forget it's the problem, not the solution, that we need to "fall in love with." If this is the case, when someone at the top of the organization makes a suggestion, the team knows they can be as open as they have to be when determining the feasibility of the suggested solution–aware as they are of what the data is telling them. It's what I call being data-inspired.

What I Learned As I Adapted the Concepts at Corporations

I realized that in order for lean startups to operate, three things must happen:

- Avoid the silo trap.
- Focus on business outcomes.
- Connect current disparate initiatives into a bigger picture where lean startup is the engine.

When I introduced lean startup in organizations, I avoided the silo trap by providing an end-to-end vision. Rather than invest in lean startup as a separate value-promoting initiative, I focused on the business benefits of an integrative solution that included agile, scaled agile, Lean UX, design thinking, and other so-called legacy methods in place such as Six Sigma. I constructed a strategic operating model that abstracted the relationships between the various frameworks used in the organization.

As an example, at an insurance company I worked alongside the leadership team to integrate the various frameworks they had in place, such as Six Sigma, Agile Scrum and Kanban, Scaled Agile and Lean UX. They were contemplating introducing Lean Startup into the mix. We ideated and synthesized the unifying model and offered a comprehensive design of framework relationships and interface deliverables. **We aligned the deliverables with the lean startup engine that was implemented.**

■ **Best Practice**   What is your strategic operating model? Lean startup as a delivery mechanism can succeed only once a strategic operating model has been synthesized; otherwise the disparate silos frameworks will collide and clash, and the transformation will fail.

The following is an example of using this framework in a large big data company. This company wanted to research opportunities in streamlining processes, delivering results cross-functionally across multiple groups and departments. Another goal was to improve customer satisfaction and automate processes as much as possible. There were also ever-increasing regulatory requirements, like the European privacy rules on how data on businesses and individuals can be obtained and stored, which represented an ongoing opportunity for this business. The objective was to provide the highest value customer service in the most efficient way. The company created an approach of empowering employees in solution-finding while maintaining continuous and close relationships with the customers.

In this company, I launched a framework to deal with enterprise-wide challenges; we called it Lean Pilots. At first, we set out to apply lean Six Sigma principles and practices (it seemed the most natural structure for problem solving), but when we realized we needed a faster way to deliver change and an immediate feedback loop, we decided to introduce elements of agile. In essence, we ran bounded experiments with combining the two methodologies. Finally, we introduced lean startup ideas—a direct result of us realizing our aim was to learn as much and as quickly as possible from our customers.

Our Lean Pilot framework implemented lean Six Sigma DMAIC[4] cycle at cadence using a Scrum framework. DMAIC is a data-driven quality strategy used to improve processes. It is an integral part of a Six Sigma initiative, but in general can be implemented as a standalone quality improvement procedure.

From the Scrum perspective, it meant that for every iteration (sprint), one or more high priority feature from the improvement backlog (may be related to business process improvement, process automation, or product enhancement) was implemented and then measured to define whether the result met Lean Pilot's success criteria. This is where the lean startup experimentation concept came into play. If the measure brought performance to a predefined level, we persevered; if the result was unfavorable, the hypothesis was invalidated and the team pivoted the next sprint to implement the next highest priority measure. This provided a safe and fast way to fail and ensured high efficiency in validating any assumptions.

---

[4]DMAIC is an acronym for Define, Measure, Analyze, Improve, and Control. It refers to a data-driven improvement cycle used for improving, optimizing, and stabilizing business processes and designs.

This combination, coupled with the cross-organizational and cross-functional nature of modern-day impediments, made this lean-agile framework so powerful.

The first step in the framework was the creation of a cross-functional team, to whom we gave the power to make decisions. To prioritize the work, we used lean (in particular, the Pareto 80/20 rule), while we relied on an agile framework Scrum to give the team the ability to define milestones and deliver value at regular intervals.

■ **Tip** Brainstorm with your team to identify the biggest opportunities within your company where the Lean Pilot framework would be applicable. Get buy-in to launch such a pilot within your enterprise to apply lean startup principles in practice. Relentlessly prioritize and measure results as you go, and you will be surprised with the outcome.

Our lean initiatives were a join-by-invitation, which meant that we could spread the methodology organically across the business. Besides self-organizing team members who were empowered to plan and execute their work, we maintained two other Scrum roles: Scrum Master and the Product Owner.

Product Owners who were subject matter experts and influencers within the corporation led teams and prioritized the work that had to be done, in collaboration with a large group of stakeholders. Scrum Masters were servant leaders who supported the team from an execution perspective; they established the cadence, provided tools, maintained process, and removed obstacles of any kind to enable the team to deliver smoothly and collaboratively. Both Product Owners and Scrum Masters were well-respected across the business and could be considered change agents within the company.

Multiple business goals were achieved by the Lean Pilot teams. One of our Lean Pilots focused on contract automation and making doing business with us easier for our customers. We wanted to increase the number of contracts signed electronically, and indeed in five months we saw a spike in the number, from 31 to 56%. Another example was the vendor management process with decreased cycle time from vendor onboarding from 17 to 9 days in nine three-week sprints ("sprint" is an iteration in Scrum) and then going down to 6 (industry standard is 10). Other Lean Pilots included compliance, procurement, global rollouts, and the core of our business, the data. We then implemented this framework in optimizing the product launch process, from ideation and development to marketing and sales. There is no limit to areas where the Lean Pilot framework proves to be beneficial.

In sum, Lean Pilot provided a way for us to rapidly resolve internal inefficiencies and to provide long-term solutions. Normally, the Lean Pilots we ran were related to process inefficiencies, customer dissatisfaction, or multiple types of waste in end-to-end processes. In each case, these pilots included analysis and ongoing experiments performed by self-organizing teams and were measured in short intervals to decide whether the team should pivot or persevere, a direct link to the lean startup practices.

■ **Best Practice** Value stream mapping is an undervalued lean technique that allows for alignment in addition to process optimization. It visualizes the "cost of delay:" the cost of not doing something vs. the cost of doing it. It helps to surface gaps in analyzing efficiencies and workflows (in other words, the whole process may take hours but handovers and related wait times take weeks and even months).

Identify Metrics That Matter

Metrics and Measures Drive Behavior

Metrics are used to drive improvements and help businesses focus their people and resources on what's important. Moreover, metrics drive decision-making: what should the company concentrate on, what objectives should be prioritized higher than others, how is the enterprise progressing towards the objective, and what measures are required for course correction? These are the questions that every enterprise faces. No resources are limitless, so on top of the necessity to focus on the highest priority objectives aligned with a company's mission, as discussed in Chapter 3, a company needs an effective mechanism to identify early and objective signs of failure and to assess root causes, whether they are unrealistic expectations, resourcing and skill-related challenges, or poor self-organization and leadership.

© Michael Nir 2018
M. Nir, *The Pragmatist's Guide to Corporate Lean Strategy*,
https://doi.org/10.1007/978-1-4842-3537-9_5

What I Read

Metrics are the keys to success for several reasons:

1. Success is defined via metrics. Agilists writing acceptance criteria for the user stories are well familiar with the INVEST mnemonic. T in this mnemonic refers to "Testable;" the acceptance criteria must provide measures of achieving results. If the goal is to improve customer satisfaction, this goal may be never achieved if we strive to an unstated measure of customer satisfaction. However, if we agree to bring the NPS (net promoter score) up to 8 out of 10, we know when to stop the project and consider it a success. Similarly, if we agree to reduce cycle time for a measured baseline from 10 days to 5, we create a **shared understanding of what success looks like**. The concept of SMART goals emphasizes the role of metrics in aligning the business to customer needs and shareholder satisfaction.

2. In order to make decisions, metrics must be objective. In numerous instances, decisions are by the highest ranking decision maker or the loudest voice in the room.[1] By having a measure of success, we remove ambiguity from the decision-making process.

3. Metrics must be actionable by providing enough information to course correct. If customer satisfaction is not improving as expected, we need to dig deeper into the root cause to understand what drives customer satisfaction and how it impacts the business overall. Eric Ries refers to it as the "three As": actionable, accessible, and auditable.

Metrics and measurements drive behavior. Following a study I once read, I decided to experiment. I placed a plastic board with the word **waste measurement** above a trash bin next to a production line that was having quality issues. I said nothing in advance and I didn't share any message about why the board was placed and what management was planning to do with the measurements. The waste in the trash bin was quickly reduced and the quality of production improved.

---

[1]Nir Michael, Agile Decisions: Driving Effective Agile Decisions in Business, CreateSpace Independent Publishing Platform; 2 edition (July 15, 2014).

Every time a measurement is put in place, behavior changes. I am not advocating that you do the same, since often the behavioral changes are not foreseen; however, I want to emphasize the impact measurements have in driving behavior. Actually, sometimes the measurement can run contrary to the desired outcome and many organizations have horror stories of measurements that went awry.

In another organization I worked at, recognition and awards were a big part of the culture. The CTO would come to the desk of an employee who had been nominated for an award and hand her the letter of nomination. There were company-wide awards with mini-movies produced in multiple funny formats, and the recognized employees were flown into the headquarters quarterly to collect these awards as a culmination of a company's town hall.

What's wrong with this approach? Recognition is an important part of company culture and employee motivation. There was nothing wrong with it, except for there was no way to nominate a team, only an individual. As a result, it was not uncommon for people to take credit for work performed by others or to pursue initiatives on their own rather than contributing to the work of the team they were part of. It took a while to change this culture, and eventually the company opened award nominations to teams in addition to individuals.

In each case, the key to establishing metrics is: when establishing metrics, the first rule is to promote behaviors the company would like to establish. Besides quantifying business outcomes, metrics shape the culture.

It is also important to balance leading and lagging metrics in decision-making. The following are some examples:

- **Leading indicators**: Number of innovations, number of patents, customer satisfaction, brand recognition, cycle time from start to completion of a workflow, growth in new markets

- **Lagging indicators**: Net revenue, revenue growth, return on net assets, operating income growth, team velocity, PI predictability measure

Leading indicators allow you to predict success or failure, and allow you to be proactive in applying validated learning to day-to-day business operations. Lagging indicators are important in making decisions on whether to continue to pursue the course of the business or switch investment into different areas.

Metrics collected may be different depending on the nature of the business and the stage it is in. For example, for an existing business, it is important to assess market value, net promoter score, and revenue. For a new business, it is more important to assess growth and increasing efficiency (as it will lead to profitability). Dave McClure's "pirate metrics" provide a set of validated metrics for any service-oriented business that represents customer behavior: Activation, Acquisition, Retention, Revenue, Referral (AARRR).[2]

Finally, it is important to realize that not all organizations are metrics-driven. Opponents of metrics frequently state that metrics can be easily gamed. As always, the truth is in between. Obviously, the way we measure data influences the numbers. For example, even such an objective metric as the cycle time (how long something takes from start to finish) can be gamed by how the cycle is defined (e.g. if a process to address a customer request starts when the request is made by the customer or when it has been prioritized for execution by a service desk; the first could expose weeks of "gap" time while the second could take hours and even minutes).

However, how this metric is defined and measured can be controlled and agreed upon. Eric Ries refers to it as "auditable" metrics, meaning that everyone involved in the initiative should be able to see the reports and understand them. Data has to be collected in a uniform and transparent way. This is another key to successful metrics that drive informed decisions: mapping metrics to a limited number (3-5) of pain points and measuring each parameter consistently in the agreed-upon way with a clear measure of success. I have orchestrated numerous ways of automating metrics collection using a number of workflow tools, lifecycle management, and data virtualization tools. If there is one investment a company can afford, I would advise to start with this one. If there is no way to measure progress objectively, no initiative will be successful (for the reason of not being able to measure success or failure).

What Happened When I Tried Implementing in Big Corporations

Large enterprises rarely argue the value of metrics. However, there are two frequent problems:

1. **Failure to recognize the value of metrics as "validated learning:"** One of the lean startup principles. Metrics are not a reason to punish employees for failing but rather an opportunity to make business decisions as early in the game as possible.

---

[2]Inc., Walter Chen, "AARRR! Dave McClure's 'Pirate Metrics' and The Only Five Numbers That Matter," www.inc.com/walter-chen/aarrr-dave-mcclure-s-pirate-metrics-and-the-only-five-numbers-that-matter.html, 2016.

2. **Vanity metrics:** In a large test prep company, there were about 20 parameters that were measured around the organization: student progress test by test, student and parent satisfaction, teacher availability, individual tutor rating, UI efficiency, rating against competitors, and many others. A lot of time and effort was invested in data collection, analysis, and resulting actions. At the same time, the company was not addressing the changing nature of the educational landscape and the major disruption happening in the education industry by Khan Academy, Coursera, and open MIT courses. The large number of parameters were distorting the real picture and impeding leadership from decision making.

It is important to collect the right metrics to inform sound business decisions and drive the desired behaviors, and as simply and clearly as possible. For metrics that do not inform the right decisions or address the root cause, lean startup uses the term "vanity metrics:" numbers that look as good as possible but do not reveal the truth and prevent the right business decisions rather than inform them.[3]

▦ **Anti-Pattern** A big data company that providing financial services was concerned that its large-scale initiatives, though deemed successful, were not bringing the expected business success. As a coach and consultant, I was initially tempted to dig deeper into how business goals were set up and how the pain points and business opportunities were identified. I spent limited time reviewing business initiatives, customer feedback, and company balance sheets. However, then I looked at the percentage of successful projects. Despite lower industry averages, a whopping 90% of this company's projects were reported as successful. There were, however, multiple surprises when a project that had been reported as "green" throughout delivery in fact failed miserably when it was supposed to be delivered or, even worse, when it was delivered to production. Upon further analysis, I found out that the company had a history of firing leaders and team members who were involved in the projects that were reported as failing. As a result, no one wanted to be the messenger in delivering honest and transparent metrics throughout execution. What's the moral of this story? If there is no safe space, any metric is questionable.

---

[3]Eric Ries, *The Startup Way. How Modern Companies Use Entrepreneurial Management to Transform Culture and Drive Long-Term Growth* (New York, NY: Currency, 2017).

As an opposite example, an engineering leader in a health industry giant I worked at decided to take engineering practices within his organization to the next level. To do so, he formulated a number of objectives: implement test automation, move applications to the cloud, increase component-based system design including microservices, and implement a number of other objectives specific to his area of responsibility. Despite the standard advice of limiting the number of objectives, he decided on a total of 12 annual goals he wanted this organization to achieve. He felt that it was important to make the progress visible, so he created a board (a simple PowerPoint slide with a 12x12 matrix with each cell colored red, yellow, or green plus a physical board in each physical location of his highly distributed team) that he called "Get to Green" and created clear measurements for each: what red, yellow, and green looked like for each division within his organization. Then he invited a representative from each division to form a continuous improvement group that baselined each of the divisions and started meeting monthly to review progress.

At this point, you might think that there was some unhealthy competition in this group or that the reviews were not objective. Nothing like that! I was invited to facilitate these conversations and each of these meetings resulted in a valuable conversation between professionals who shared advice, supported consistent tooling, training, and methodology, and moved from being primarily "red" to being uniformly "green" within one year on each of these 12 parameters—all while the teams were competing, celebrating "getting to green" in each of the 12 parameters, and gamifying this journey on top of learning new skills and implementing new technologies.

■ **Best Practice**   Jeff Patton[4] discusses **output-outcome-impact** metrics in *User Story Mapping*. The four disciplines[5] of execution emphasize lead metrics rather than lag metrics. I found that the most effective metrics that lead to enterprise success are a combination of both approaches, the so-called **impact lead** metrics. Contrast that with what organizations traditionally focus on when implementing agile (team velocity metric) or when implementing scaled agile (train velocity metric). In both cases, the metric is a lag output metric; it is a delayed indicator of performance. On top of which, it is an output measure; high or low team velocity tell us nothing about the actual outcome of the delivered work and in no way informs us of the impact that the delivered work item has.

---

[4]Jeff Paton, *User Story Mapping: Discover the Whole Story, Build the Right Product* (Springfield, MO: O'Reilly, 2014).
[5]Chris McChesney, Sean Covey, and Jim Huling, *The 4 Disciplines of Execution: Achieving Your Wildly Important Goals* (New York, NY: Free Press, 2016).

What I Learned As I Adapted the Concepts at Corporations

Bigger organizations are inherently different than smaller organizations, a truth that is easy to forget. As a result, these lessons from lean startup are often adapted to organizational realities:

1. In the rush to transform the organization, we often forget to ask ourselves what metrics would show success and what would be lead metrics that would guide us, helping us to know we are headed in the right direction.

2. Many agile transformations embrace team velocity as one of the three top metrics and promise executives an ongoing improvement of velocity. One may ask why velocity is the wrong metric. Actually, it is not! Focusing on velocity as a metric is similar to focusing on output rate in production; it is a wrong metric to meaure and celebrate. However since it is so easy to measure, organizations prefer to focus on it rather than explore leading metrics that are impactfull.

3. In a recent scaled agile implementation, senior executives joined the big room planning event and asked the teams why their velocity was low and how they could produce more in the next quarter. When we analyzed the work the teams were producing, we were concerned that the work itself was the wrong work. The teams were focused on developing whimsical requests by key business owners rather than the core functionality of the products. **By focusing on velocity (the team output) we failed to notice that we were not creating the required outputs that would lead us to sustained impacts in the market**. I found this to be a recurring pattern in big organizations. Actually, the bigger the organization and the more silos in place, the more metrics that are local lagging output driven rather than metrics that shape the success of the organization.

4. We learned that we needed a framework to validate the metrics, both internal and external. We classified metrics as output-outcome-impact and examined the metrics currently in place. We broke them down into categories. Most metrics were internal output lag metrics. Velocity is a good example: it measures the rate of task completion, so once it is measured we can no longer affect it. We found that more than 75% of the metrics were output metrics and 90% were lag metrics.

5. We challenged ourselves to develop a few lead metrics that measured outcome and impact.

■ **Tip**   Reflect: What are the meaningful metrics in your organization? What data is currently collected? How does it drive desired behaviors? Which are vanity numbers and which are meaningful, in your opinion? How does this inform decision-making? Is it visible throughout the organization? How does it cascade throughout all structures?

Once you answer these questions, identify any improvements throughout the organization and think of how it collects and uses data. Share these ideas with your peers and the management team.

Pivot or Persevere

Get the Lean Engine Going

A pivot is a change in strategy without a change in vision.

—Eric Ries, author known for his popular book on the
Lean Startup movement[1]

In my experience, defining the right objectives and a way to measure progress is the foundation. What defines success, though, is the ability to act fast based on this information. How do enterprises react if their transformation does not achieve the agreed-upon results in the defined period of time? Either by course correcting and pursuing the original objective (persevering) or by pivoting and pursing new objectives based on the learning from the failure.

Do you remember a funny episode from *Friends* where Ross, when directing the moving of a couch up a stairwell, yells "pivaaat" repeatedly, without understanding what the word actually means? No wonder the couch eventually got stuck. Similarly, large corporations frequently get stuck without understanding when and where they need to pivot or pursue their original business, like Kodak or Blockbuster not being able to respond to the new

---

[1]Eric Ries, *The Startup Way. How Modern Companies Use Entrepreneurial Management to Transform Culture and Drive Long-Term Growth* (New York, NY: Currency, 2017).

© Michael Nir 2018
M. Nir, *The Pragmatist's Guide to Corporate Lean Strategy*,
https://doi.org/10.1007/978-1-4842-3537-9_6

market conditions. The question of when to pivot and when to hold the line is the difference between success and failure for many businesses. How does company leadership know it's time to pivot? How do they define the new objective? When is it the right time?

What I Read

Once the business strategy is established and success criteria are defined, execution progresses incrementally, with validated learning occuring every step of the way. How does the enterprise leadership know that the direction is unrealistic or not feasible, so that they can pursue other opportunities and redefine the finish line? There is a lot of research on this topic, my favorite one being the collection of three criteria:

- Users do not like/use the product.
- Employee motivation is low.
- The market does not respond/is not ready.

In a blog providing four criteria to define whether it is time to pivot,[2] Bernard Moon also provides several successful pivots whose original ideas used validated learning in achieving future success:

- Burbn, a location-based HTML5 app ➤ Instagram
- Game Neverending, an online video game (MMORPG) ➤ Flickr
- Tune in Hook Up, a video dating site ➤ YouTube
- PDA payments (Palm) ➤ PayPal's web payments
- Odeo, a podcasting platform ➤ Twitter
- Animation tools ➤ Pixar's animation studio
- Memory chips ➤ Intel's microprocessors

Sometimes the product won't be right and sometimes the market won't be ready, but the bottom line is that there is an early time to pivot: before the signs become clear outside the company, explore new opportunities, foster internal innovation, research potential acquisitions—anything instead of trying to pursue the original vision, which is not working. The concept of rapid experimentation driven by pivot-or-persevere decisions based on impact metrics is the key to success at the corporate level as well as for early startups.

---

[2]Venturebeat, Bernard Moon, "4 signs that your startup is ready to pivot," https://venturebeat.com/2013/01/11/pivot/, 2013.

What Happened When I Tried Implementing in Big Corporations

A large educational company I worked for recognized the need to pivot later than most major market players, and the leadership made a decision to pursue market opportunities as fast as they could. Switching from a traditional face-to-face tutoring schema, they create online courses, apps, and mentoring sessions post-2010—way too late to catch up with the growing digital education market. It was clear that the company needed to pivot but not clear how, given its 75-year legacy and vast experience in traditional tutoring and small-class test prep education.

To sustain its business, the company initially relied on internal product and engineering resources and created many powerful mobile apps that were well received by the market. This was accomplished through internal innovation and customer-centric thinking. However, in doing so, it was were still catching up with the market and new competitors who were well ahead of them, acquiring their customer base on a growing scale.

What was the next step in pivoting this business? As you learned from Chapter 2, the company had to start with a customer in mind. What was the market segment that had significant problems the company could solve? What was the optimal way to address the problems?

Having these questions in mind, the company's leadership decided to tap into the unlimited potential of the startup world and partnered with the Techstars accelerator to host educational startups. It also acquired a social and adaptive learning platform that provided question banks for educational testing. Finally, it formed several startup ventures on its own, including one that covered an obvious gap while pivoting away from its traditional market of college applicants: the core of this business was helping its students, recent college graduates experiencing challenges in finding jobs, to get education in a high-demand field and to support their further job search.

The strategy of diversifying its experiments proved successful, although the company was not able to get the social learning platform off the ground despite significant investment. It is hard to say why this pivot, which seemed to be a perfect market fit, failed miserably within the first year of acquisition (much longer than necessary, since early signs of a failure were present). Most likely it was a combination of corporate leaders who lacked customer-focused mentality, lack of motivation, and poor acquisition strategy. That said, the job-seeking pivot worked very well and gave many people an opportunity to find a job and learn a new profession, and it allowed the parent company to sustain the disruption. An interesting addition to this story is that the professional career development business started as a programming/engineering course and rapidly pivoted to data sciences/machine learning specialization, which allowed it to avoid competition with cheaper offshore talent and address an empty niche in the job market.

What I Learned As I Adapted the Concepts in Corporations

Neil Patel provides a 12-step guide to pivoting,[3] which contains the following steps:

1. Realize when your plan isn't working.

2. Come up with a list of possible reasons why it's not working.

3. Gain a fresh perspective on your long-term goals and vision for the business.

4. Revise those goals and vision as necessary.

5. Come up with a list of ideas that will help you to accomplish those goals.

6. Develop a clearly defined plan.

7. Define the numbers or signs that will gauge the success of your new plan.

8. Forget the previous plan.

9. Explain the new plan to the team.

10. Embrace the new plan.

11. Watch the metrics.

12. Rinse and repeat.

These 12 steps provide a practical sequence to lean startup's pivot-or-persevere model. The most important key to success is not the process; as usually, it's people-related. This value is called *courage*. The courage to move forward at triple speed at early signs of success and persevere in achieving the goal if success criteria are met. The courage to pivot from a once-exciting idea to a different one based on validated learning, now smarter and equipped with newly acquired learning. In either case, time is of an essence, and courage is the fuel.

---

[3] *Huffington Post*, Neil Patel, "How to Pivot: A 12-Step Guide to Pivoting Your Startup," www.huffingtonpost.com/neil-patel/how-to-pivot-a-12step-gui_b_9560326.html, March 30, 2016,

When I presented the ideas of a pivot, it resonated well within the organization. However, implementing a pivot is a challenge. A large Fortune 100 client of mine has a robust culture program. They teach it, implement it and celebrate it. When one of the IT programs they managed hit a dead end we facilitated a retrospective and reviewed the five values that were the corner stone of the cultural program. Courage wasn't one of them. Upon further inspection I argued that the values could lead to a culture of complacency and mediocrity since they promoted behaviours of accpetance and consensus rather than risk taking and speaking up. A senior manager at the company shared with me that you could recieve a bonus as long as you: 'played the cultural game' so to speak. Pivoting as a behaviour was not something that the cultural program espoused. Without courage as a value the cultural program was missing a valuable driver for pivoting.

A pivot is a change; and in bigger organizations, a pivot impacts more people than it does in startups.

We had to identify methods to present a pivot in a positive way, embracing the validated learning and following through with the change. We found that Kotter's eight steps to change were limiting us had we been required to implement them for every pivot. Additionally, the bigger the team involved, the more we got mired in communicating the pivot.

While small startups can pivot themselves on a daily basis, in bigger businesses we learned we had to integrate the concept of the pivot into the operating model. We had to explain to the organization the accepted amount of pivots in a certain timeframe; in other words, how many pivots were allowed in a given timeframe. We found that the concepts of a pivot were not necessarily foreign to the portfolio management team and the program managemenet office. Traditional product development frameworks introduce phase gates to support a GO/NO GO decision at various intervals of the development process. In practice though these become mere administrative hurdles to overcome as the project or program progresses towards completion and the product is released to the market. Often the phase gates involve only a review of documentation rather than evidence based feedback to a working model of the product. This is where pivoting provides a different framework than the traditional phase gate approach. The decision to pivot must be based on empirical validation evidence (relevant lead-impact metrics). This evidence is collected from real consumers (representing the selected persona) who interact with a partial solution - an MVP. The MVP integrates important and uncertain assumptions that we identified enabling us to meaure true alignment with our vision. These pivot decisions are in line with our vision and mission to deliver the right products and features that would delight our customers. The framework brings together concepts from various schools of thought - thus it is crucial to Synthesize an Integrative Operating Model.

Otherwise pivoting, which is at the heart of a successful lean enterprise implementation will not be truly accepted as an option and will be viewed as a failure rather than as validated learning.

■ **Best Practice**   Make pivoting a celebrated event. Bigger organizations are reluctant to pivot and see a pivot as a threat. So lower the danger, reduce the impact, and demonstrate the benefits of the pivot.

As I shared in the beginning of this book, my goal is to equip you, the reader, with everything you need to implement a holistic approach to enterprise-level lean agile transformation. The first section described what I learned, often the hard way, when adapting lean agile concepts at organizations bigger than 500 employees. I reviewed the fundamentals of the lean startup framework, as well as agile, lean, design thinking, and Lean UX frameworks to analyze the five key fundamentals of success for any enterprise transformation. I also analyzed examples from my experience that exhibit patterns and anti-patterns related to implementing the framework. In the following section, I review how to apply these examples to the reality of an enterprise transformation.

■ **Tip**   Think of two well-known examples of companies that successfully pivoted and reinvented themselves. Answer the following questions: What did they do well? Was it timing, luck, finding the right market, flexibility, acquisition strategy, and/or employee and customer focus?

Next, think of two companies that did not survive the disruption and answer the question: What if those companies had pivoted? Try to envision the future for Kodak, Blockbuster, Nokia, and many others who did not pivot despite market demand. Share your thoughts with a colleague and discuss the strategy of pivoting vs. pursuing the original business model.

Five Techniques to Succeed

In the second section of this book, I bring the concepts and practical steps into a single framework. I offer you a framework, not a one-size-fits-all methodology. You will have a set of tools and techniques with well-defined values and best practices while retaining the flexibility of your implementation. You will be able to present these ideas to senior management for their buy-in as a single thought-through framework and you can orchestrate implementation at scale while avoiding common pitfalls. This section contains templates that you can use in your organization to orchestrate experimentation, reduce risk, anticipate customer needs, and predict success of your products before you start building them.

I opted to present the information in this section from the viewpoint of a day in the life of a pragmatic corporate lean strategy change leader. My initial approach was that of a framework-by-framework analysis of tools and techniques to succeed; however, I felt that synthesizing the information from the day-in-the-life perspective would provide a comprehensive map of the step-by-step plan for corporate lean strategy and execution. The day-in-the-life perspective also enables getting started faster and delivering results quicker.

You'll read about the following five techniques to succeed, progress, and change, along with the implementation timeline:

- Define the mission.
- Identify customer personas.
- Implement the prototype MVP and program training.
- Run experiments with customers to validate your hypotheses.
- Pivot or persevere in a build-measure-learn cycle.

I develop a daily schedule that includes the above five techniques to succeed and their focus in the implementation timeline of the first 30 days, the first 90 days, and the first 12 months.

First 30 Days

Leading, Training, and Coaching

You've just received the mandate to roll out lean in the enterprise. What does your day look like?

Table 7-1 details the percentage of time allocated to various activities in the first 30 days of a lean enterprise rollout in the enterprise.

Table 7-1. Time Spent on Activities–First 30 days

Activity	Time Spent	Comments
Define vision	50%	Collaborative vision definition
Identify customer personas	10%	Focus on outside-in point of view
Prototype MVP and program training	25%	Train executive leadership
Run experiments	10%	Prepare for experiments
Pivot or persevere	5%	Ideate potential pivots

Define Vision

Most of the first 30 days are spent defining, articulating, communicating, reviewing, and validating the vision.

I suggest collaborating with senior executives from various organizational business units to crystalize the message. Using collaborative interactive approaches is the best method for creating an agreed-upon vision that is

© Michael Nir 2018
M. Nir, *The Pragmatist's Guide to Corporate Lean Strategy*,
https://doi.org/10.1007/978-1-4842-3537-9_7

sustainable. Calling these vision meetings *workshops* and having the participants actively participate with the guidance of an external facilitator produces the wanted results. *Postcard from the future*, which I mentioned previously, is an inclusive exercise through which a two-year vision can be obtained.

More often than not, there are already many frameworks in place and you need to examine them and identify how they map into the lean startup framework in the enterprise. The postcard workshop can be used to initiate the discussion of how the lean engine drives the organization to the results depicted in the vision.

The various frameworks I discussed earlier tend to be clustered in silos. There may be agile for development, scaled agile for larger development teams, Lean UX for designers and consumer experience experts, DEVOPS for operations, 4DX for business operations, Lean Six Sigma for quality improvement initiatives; often we are missing the integrating function. To be successful, we must articulate the lean engine and its relationship to the existing frameworks.

The vision should provide an overarching compelling description of how we will be different once we adopt the lean mindset. In figuring out the direction, I suggest an outside-in view. What will be different from a consumer standpoint? What will the new consumer experience look like?

The next step is to understand how the various frameworks adopted in the past support the outside-in vision.

Consider a Boston-based software organization that recently doubled in size and was catering to new and bigger enterprises. The original vision was one of survival; however, post-IPO and as it expanded, it was figuring out how lean and business agility fit within its structure. The company was implementing agile in engineering and in operations; however, it wasn't seeing the promised benefits. It was constantly shifting priorities; roadmaps were created every six months and then scrapped and redone. Operations were handled in a constant crisis mode where heroes were recognized by their ability to resolve crises ad hoc without providing a longer-term remedy. The sales focus was that of closing contracts rather than engagement with consumers with long-term orientation. The lean engine for growth was missing; products were not validated with the market. In other words, the company spent six to nine months developing products without validating them with consumers. The list of requirements that was handed down to development was based on best-guess scenarios developed by the leadership team. When a hurricane hit Florida or wild fires in California roared, the company was ill-equipped to support emergency operations since the product vision was disparate. Its vision was not supported by the frameworks it had in place and not validated by the various business units. The agile delivery system produced results; however, it produced the wrong results because it was missing a validating structure.

▨ **Tip** My recommendation for the senior vice president of product development at this organization was to increase the UX team and tie user experience to product development. At the same time, I suggested that the separate engineering and operations departments, which were managed as two silos, be united under one leader. The lean engine became the driver for product development and validation, reducing the time from initial ideation to first MVP validated.

Figure 7-1 describes a compelling vision image that I developed for one of my clients. Following the concepts presented in Jim Collin's *Good to Great*[1] book, we first identified the team that drove towards the vision. In other words, we figured who was driving the bus and who was on the bus, and then we identified the behavior we expected riders to have as well as the minimal skillsets needed. The bus was headed to the vision; in this case, for this financial services company, it was a new digital consumer experience. The team on the bus utilized scaled agile to deliver results; they were also trained in human-centric design to figure out what an outside-in view was. They were supported by corporate oversight–the bird. They were supported by business architecture–the cat.[2] The lean engine was used to break the roadblocks that they encountered by removing traditional silos and validating assumptions on the way to attaining the vision. The lean engine focused on directing the bus towards the vision, to avoid the bus going back to the traditional way of work, which is represented by a road that curves back to the original starting point.

The client used the vision shown in Figure 7-1 when articulating the program to both internal and external stakeholders and the organization at large. The image was posted in the collaborative open space where executives met for vision and mission discussions. The vision also helped in clarifying the relationship between the various frameworks they had already adopted.

---

[1]Jim Collins, *Good to Great: Why Some Companies Make the Leap and Others Don't*, (New York, NY: HarperBusiness, 2001).
[2]The cat, since we likened the architecture to Schrodinger's cat, which has to be both on the bus and also provide clarity in business architecture intersections.

Figure 7-1. Communicate a compelling vision image when describing the future state. (Source: Graphic design by Hen Nir. © Sapir Consulting US LLC 2017, www.michaelnir.com)

Identify Customer Personas

During the first 30 days of the corporate lean strategy and implementation program, the lean leader starts discussing the persona that they will be focusing on. Actually, in most organizations the inside-out mindset prevails and little has been done in the past, if at all, to promote an outside-in understanding. Therefore the initial activities related to this task are strategic in nature.

While startups have been trained to adopt an outside-in view and rapid validation with the consumer, bigger organizations hardly ever do. The novel approach discussed in the successful Google ventures *Sprint: How to Solve Big Problems and Test New Ideas in Just Five Days*[3] has started a movement towards rapid validation; however, my experience has shown it is limited in scope. The design focus of these efforts creates a local solution that is not integrated into the culture of the enterprise. I believe that the missing element

---

[3]Jake Knapp, John Zeratsky, and Braden Kowitz, *Sprint: How to Solve Big Problems and Test New Ideas in Just Five Days* (New York, NY: Simon & Schuster, 2016).

is the essential orientation towards an outside-in point of view. Identifying customer persona activities in the first 30 days are spent on reflecting how the enterprise presently focuses on the consumers; usually this results in increased awareness that the current operational behaviors by-and-large are not driven by an outside-in view.

■ **Anti-Pattern** There are still many organizations that resist an outside-in orientation. While currently it may seem that companies can survive by being internal-centric, it doesn't seem a viable long-term strategy for most. Seth Godin's *We Are All Weird: The Rise of Tribes and the End of Normal*[4] makes the case to the profound change we are witnessing to a consumer outside-in orientation.

Without a true outside-in focus, identifying customer personas results in a tactical exercise that is confined to user experience experts involving a small elite group of like-minded thinkers. It fails to impact the broader organization. In order to succeed with lean in the enterprise, the first step in defining the personas is gaining a better understanding of how the organization thinks about the consumers:

- What are the various interactions with the consumers?

- What are the held beliefs about the consumers?

- What are descriptions that internal employees have of the consumers?

- Which words are used to describe the consumers?

Big organizations and corporations are characterized by little interaction with customers both internal and external. Take, for example, a Boston-based company invested heavily in user experience design, employing a team of 40 experts researching user personas. They ran an innovation lab that focused on innovative product design and developed creative software solutions to fulfill persona needs. The challenge, though, was the strategic orientation of customer-centric thinking. The personas served in tactical product design but were not a driver in bigger product thinking.

While the personas were well thought and articulated, the outside-in thinking was missing. This company spent three years creating a state-of-the-art configurable online editor. They had a team of 30 engineers and product designers leading the effort. The program received priority for every product design activity during the three years.

---

[4]Seth Godin, *We Are All Weird: The Rise of Tribes and the End of Normal* (New York, NY: Portfolio Penguin, 2015).

When the new software editor was release with much fanfare, the impact was dismal. As I described elsewhere, the 30% rule was observed. Only 30% of the consumers were happy with the new editor. This begs the question, why? When we engaged in a root cause analysis we found that while the product employed state-of-the-art engineering, it was detached from the personas that were researched, analysed, and printed on large canvas boards in the engineering work space. It seemed that the persona generation, creativity, and innovation was a separate effort that wasn't integrated into how the rest of the organization was thinking. Persona development was a one-time activity that lacked integration into the required outside-in thinking. As a result, while the consumers weren't happy with the old editor, the new editor provided too many options and encumbered the mental decision-making process, thus many consumers opted to remain with the previous editing experience.

Anti-Pattern   Inside-out thinking in this company was widespread. The engineers blamed the low user adoption of the new editor on the lack of technological savviness on the part of the consumers. That's what I referred to in the introduction as a "bad smell."

Summarizing: The first 30 days are not about discussing who is our customer and creating a well-designed colorful depiction of our main customer; rather, it is about engaging the organization at large in a collaborative discussion about how we presently serve our consumers. Is the approach we are currently employing sustainable for the long term health of the enterprise? For the financial services organization mentioned previously, the answer was no! Its inside-out point of view was not sustainable if it wished to remain competitive in the insurance market.

Tip   Remember the microwave example from the introduction? What do you think companies that develop and manufacture microwaves think about their consumers? What do these companies believe the "normal" microwave persona needs? Do you think these companies are inside-out or outside-in driven?

Prototype MVP and Program Training

The corporate lean strategy and implementation program and the lean leader facilitate training to jump-start the program. Prototyping an MVP (minimal viable product) is a team activity. The training program is initially geared to bring executive members of the organization to experience first-hand the mindset shift that is required to be successful with lean thinking in the enterprise.

I recommend facilitating three to five two-day workshops in this timeframe, and each workshop should train approximately 25 participants. A rough sketch of such a workshop is detailed below.

Figure 7-2 is used to explain the lean process as part of the training program. Once the enterprise integrates this mindset, the opportunities for much faster development of the right set of features is ripe.

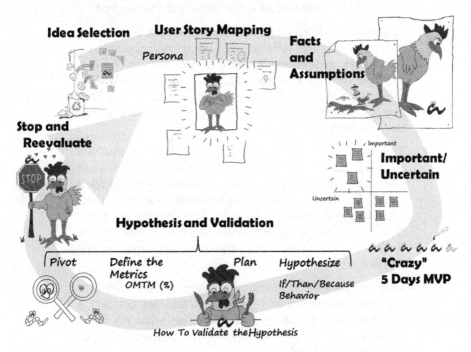

Figure 7-2. Lean startup workshop (identify the MVP) (Source: Graphic design by Hen Nir. © Sapir Consulting US LLC 2017, www.michaelnir.com)

The Lean Engine Description

The steps described in the figure are the following:

- The corporate lean strategy and implementation is a cyclical program that is intended to identify and prototype MVPs and validate the assumptions that are ingrained in these MVPs. *Ross the rooster explains the steps in the program.*

- We have many ideas in our organization. Normally we don't know which will produce an impact and which will amount to a waste if we decided to implement them. We need to create a vetting process to quickly identify which incoming ideas have merit and which should be discarded. *For example, one such idea might be to develop new chicken feed for Ross the rooster. What if we color the worms in blue? Will that be a new successful chicken feed?*

- Once we decide to move forward on an idea, we break it into steps. We use Jeff Patton's user story mapping[5] as a framework to develop ideas further. We need to create a draft persona for this exercise, since the persona affects the steps in the map. *Ross our rooster persona has thoughts, beliefs, and behaviors, and we develop them as part of user story mapping.*

- The next step is identifying facts and assumptions. We ask participants to review the user story map and write down the facts and the assumptions that are imbedded within. Then the assumptions are plotted on an important/uncertain grid. *We know for a fact that chickens eat many types of food such as apples, carrots, and crickets; however, we don't know what their reaction might be to a blue worm. Will they like it?*

- Once we identified the critical assumptions, the ones that are most important and most uncertain, we conduct a hypothetical exercise. We ask ourselves what we could possibly validate if we had only five days to spend. We call that the Crazy MVP.

- The minimal viable product is the integration of the story map, the most important and uncertain analysis, and the specific persona. It is the least amount of effort we need to invest to validate the most important and most uncertain assumption.

- The next set of steps is the development of the hypothesis, validation planning, and following through with actual validation. We'll revisit these steps later.

---

[5]Jeff Paton. *User Story Mapping: Discover the Whole Story, Build the Right Product* (Springfield, MO: O'Reilly, 2014).

■ **Best Practice** A minimal viable product is actually a mindset rather than a formula. It is the least amount of effort invested to validate an assumption. Minimal viable products are a synthesis of three elements: a persona, a user story map, and assumption analysis.

The Goal of a Lean Startup Training Program

The lean startup training program is hands-on, experiential, engaging, and impactful; it transforms individuals' traditional thinking to an iterative-assumption-validation mindset.

We identify two goals, the first explicit and the second implicit, built into the program:

Explicitly we train cross functional teams in lean startup thinking through learning-by-doing which includes ideating a project/product/feature/opportunity, pitching to a team, identifying an MVP and personas, categorizing assumptions, validation planning, and following through with a 90-day execution of the hypothesis testing, and lastly presenting the results to senior leadership. **In the first 30 days, we focus on training the leadership teams.**

Implicitly we expect participants to question the traditional approach of pushing a new project/product/feature/opportunity into the deployment pipeline without first validating assumptions, and to embrace a lean mindset. We expect that participants will internalize the lean startup concepts and transform from the traditional approach of big bang planning to an MVP assumption validation mindset.

The Objectives of the Two-Day Workshop

The following are the objectives:

- Describe the elements of the lean startup approach.
- Articulate the key benefits of using the lean startup approach.
- Practice lean, agile, and design thinking tools and techniques.
- Apply the approach to your organization.

The Concept of a Lean Startup Program

The program follows the following steps:

- Pre-workshop individual assignment: Participants are tasked with ideating a project from their work environment that they want to explore using the lean framework.

- Workshop: Two-day, hands-on, experiential workshop

- Workshop first evening reflection: Participants are tasked with a short exercise, reviewing the product of the first day of the workshop.

- Workshop team assignment: The team works on a selected project from their work environment throughout the second day of the workshop.

- **Team post-workshop activity: The team has 90 days to deliver validated hypothesis; the team meets weekly**.

- Team lean startup coaching: The team meets with the lean startup coach bi-weekly for 30 minutes to review progress and clear impediments.

- Team Exhibition: After 90 days, the team presents their learning, project, and possible prototype in an exhibition-style booth to senior leadership and stakeholders.

As mentioned previously, the program commences with training the executive leadership in the first 30 days.

Tip How can we validate the minimal set of features required for a microwave without investing the effort in actually manufacturing it?

Run Experiments with Customers to Validate Your Hypotheses

Few experiments are managed in the first 30 days. The training of the executive team occurs two weeks after the program kick off. Normally the executives identify several key areas that require attention; however, they don't articulate them as hypotheses and therefore they aren't ready for experimenting.

You will read more about key areas that require attention and lean pilot successes in providing solutions in section three.

The first 30 days are spent providing the rational for experimenting. I noticed that the **knee-jerk reaction of big organizations to the concept of experimenting is refuting the need for more experimentation**. In their minds, there is enough experimenting going on already and the obstacle is actually making the decision rather than collecting more data. In that sense, they are correct. Compared with startups, big organizations do have mechanisms to collect information and they collect mounds of data without ever using it; the difference is the **perspective of the scientific method and engagement with the users**.

What big enterprises really mean when they say that they experiment is not what I refer to as such. Take for example a VP of Product at a financial services company in New York; when I asked him whether he validated the need for additional features for an existing investment product, his answer was yes. He followed through by handing me a 25-page summary report of a three month survey they recently completed. The report was thorough but it missed the point since there was no direct experimentation with users. When I say *experimentation*, I mean *identifying assumptions, crafting hypothesis, and creating a test plan to validate or invalidate the hypothesis*. When executives think of experimentation, they often think of sanctioning a report completed by white coat lab teams.

■ **Anti-Pattern**   When leaders and managers in enterprises say that they always validate their assumptions, they actually mean that they run numerous surveys to collect feedback, not that they interact with users to elicit true feedback on assumptions. The surveys most often validate their preconceived views; if the surveys refute them, they often call the survey wrong and proceed with their original plan,

---

In the microwave example from the introduction, if we were tasked with rethinking the features of a microwave, we might assume that there are too many features. Our VP of Product would probably test this assumption by sending a well-thought survey to a list of users or even conduct a survey at several big malls. This approach would actually provide the wrong results. As mentioned, there is a difference between what people say they want and how they use it. Instead, We would follow through by creating an MVP and use it to observe the usability of the product. However, before we placed the MVP in the hands of users, we would preempt by asking what results we expect to observe. That's the essence of the scientific methods.

The step of calling out the results is crucial. And I can't stress this enough! Yes, organizations use various data collection tools to answers questions; however, they often miss the benchmark of **evaluating their initial assumptions in light of the data**. The thought process is foreign to how organizations normally think about problems. Therefore, in the first 30 days, the goal is to root out the prevailing thinking at the enterprise and replace it with true hypothesis validation.

Best Practice Always start experimentation by calling out the results you expect to see. **A crucial part of experimentation validation is calling out the expected result prior to conducting the experiment**.

This is easier said than done. People prefer not to call out in advance what they expect to observe since they don't want their ideas refuted. Often, when survey results return, the leaders tend to read them in light of the results they wanted to see and explain them similarly. These psychological mechanisms are well described by Nobel Prize Laureate Daniel Kahneman.[6] When they craft a hypothesis before starting experimentation, the team must clearly state what they expect to observe, and they must make sure that the person making the assumption also owns the hypothesis. Daniel Kahneman would say that by asking the team to state the expected result prior to the experiment, they are engaging in system two thinking, which will lead to better results.

Anti-Pattern I am not claiming that the same psychological mechanisms of disbelieving the results of the experiment won't happen even when the team clearly states the hypothesis before validation in a scientific approach; however, they are less likely to occur.

In the first 30 days, the executives explore what has been done in the past to validate the assumptions. There are often mounds of data and the goal is to explain why the data isn't helping in the process of creating validated learning. This is achieved by turning the assumptions into hypotheses and asking the team of executives to clearly state the behaviors they expect to discover when engaging with users.

As an example, consider the following: a major retailer was replacing one of the core payment systems it had in place for years. Normally these projects last three years and run over budget, over schedule, and deliver less than promised.

---

[6]Daniel Kahneman, *Thinking Fast and Slow* (New York, NY: Farrar, Straus and Giroux, 2013).

The CTO was rethinking the IT project approach and wanted to deliver the project incrementally. Numerous business requirements were assessed and many seemed to be reflecting legacy system thinking that was not part of the future of this organization. During the first 30 days of the lean thinking program, the executives wanted to use the approach to validate assumptions reflected in the business requirements. They mentioned a specific requirement concerning billing options. The legacy system offered billing and payment every day of the month, but to create this functionality in the new system required a considerable development effort. The CEO was adamant that the feature had to be developed since he claimed it contributed to consumer delight. Other were not so certain. The CEO had a survey supporting his claim. I used this as an opportunity to clearly state the hypothesis in a scientific approach prior to validating with consumers. Specifically, I asked the team to call out the impact to *user happiness* by offering the feature of every-day-of-the-month payment. This read as: 75% of users consider the billing option as a differentiator and thus affect the NPS score by 5 points on average. The next step was to create an experiment to validate the hypothesis. Four weeks later, the actual results showed that only 15% mildly considered the option as a nice to have with little measurable impact to NPS, which refuted the CEO's hypothesis and saved a considerable development effort.

Tip Lean thinking can be used to validate back-end system requirements, not only outward facing products, and as such can have a wider impact on how the enterprise operates.

Pivot or Persevere in a Build-Measure-Learn Cycle

The experiments are starting; little validation feedback is received in the first 30 days and thus very little is done with pivot or preserve. Often the first pivot or persevere decisions occur after 90 days.

However, we need to create readiness to pivot since organizations are reluctant to pivot and actually are afraid to pivot. The shift to a culture of embracing pivots is necessary to succeed. Since many of our product and feature decisions are wrong, as mentioned in the microwave example and the recurring pattern of waste, we must put forth an agreement to embrace pivots. All too often enterprises persevere just for the fear of stopping an ongoing operation; they rationalize the decision by saying that they invested too much already and it would be a waste to stop.

▩ **Anti-Pattern** Enterprises see a pivot as failure.

Within the first 30 days of discussions, I recommend answering questions such as

- Why is it important to pivot?

- What have we done in the past that prevented us from pivoting once we had data that validated a pivot was necessary?

- What are the various options for a pivot[7] and how relevant are they to our enterprise?

- When is it acceptable to decide to pivot?

- Who is allowed to decide to pivot?

- Where are we going to manage the assumptions, hypothesis, validation, pivot, and persevere data?

- Who will manage the data?

The answers to these questions support the creation of a mechanism to manage the ongoing build-measure-learn cycle, which I will discuss in detail in the next chapter.

▩ **Tip** Low hanging fruit: Ask the leadership team for a list of ongoing projects they would suggest pivoting or cancelling, create a combined list, and identify opportunities to quickly validate and often invalidate assumptions embedded in these projects. Make sure to first identify the original hypothesis for these projects. Make the case for using lean enterprise thinking as an approach to make go/no-go decisions at project milestones as part of portfolio management.[8]

---

[7]Pivot options are summarized in Martin Zwilling's *Forbes* article "Top 10 Ways Entrepreneurs Pivot a Lean Startup" at www.forbes.com/sites/martinzwilling/2011/09/16/ top-10-ways-entrepreneurs-pivot-a-lean-startup/#1db27b112d2b.
[8]*International Journal of Production Research*, Boaz Ronen, Thomas Lechler, and Edward Stohr, "The 25/25 Rule: Achieving More by Doing Less," Volume 50, Issue 24, 2012.

First 90 Days

Leading, Coaching, and Executing

You've spent the first 30 days invested in the lean program. Half of your time was dedicated to defining the vision, a quarter was spent training the leadership team, and the remainder was divided among creating an outside-in mindset, preparing for experiments, and ideating potential pivot opportunities. You might have already identified the stakeholders supporting the program and your adversaries.

Now that the hectic first 30 days are complete, where should you focus your efforts? Table 8-1 details the percentage of time allocated to various activities in the first 90 days of a lean agile enterprise rollout.

Table 8-1. Time Spent on Activities–First 90 Days

Activity	Time Spent	Comments
Define vision	25%	Popularize with stakeholders and gain commitment
Identify customer personas	20%	Facilitate persona focus through direct engagement with the consumer
Prototype MVP and program training	25%	Train mid-level management
Run experiments	20%	Coach team to experiment with customers
Pivot or persevere	10%	Create the safety nets; pivot from failed initial MVP results

© Michael Nir 2018

M. Nir, *The Pragmatist's Guide to Corporate Lean Strategy*,

https://doi.org/10.1007/978-1-4842-3537-9_8

Develop Vision

The vision that you've well articulated in the first 30 days is still limited. As mentioned, the organization's leaders often assume that the vision is shared merely by the fact it has been created and communicated in a town hall. That couldn't be further from the truth. Usually the vision is still nebulous in minds of both the leadership team and the organization at large. Other forces see the vision of an overarching framework that is designed to deliver value as threatening their fiefdoms. In traditional silo organizational structures, middle managers see the overarching integration of existing frameworks as invading on their authority. This holds true even for so-called agile development organizations that push back on a holistic lean engine, claiming it to be an interruption to their ongoing delivery cycle. It is also true for UX experts and designers who under the false pretense of Lean UX prefer to focus on creating complete designs without the business orientation that is driven by the lean engine. Six Sigma professionals who often focus on the quality aspect of delivery view the integrated model as belittling their quality-driven efforts.

These adversarial stakeholders are unaccepting and in disagreement with the program objective and employ manipulative means to propagate disagreement. This group is the most difficult to influence.

That said, others in the organization support the vision and understand the need for an integrative model that is united by a lean engine driven by consumer validation.

The onerous task of building enough support for the program consumes a quarter of the program's effort in the first 90 days. Following the stakeholder attitude analysis that was completed in the first 30 days, you direct your attention to building the support for the program.

Your challenge, though, is focusing on the supporters rather than the adversaries. That runs counter-intuitive to how we normally build support. Often we invest time and effort to build trust and agreement with opposing stakeholders. Practically, these might be wasted efforts, leading to the opposite result. The focus on this group develops into an openly hostile conflict that resonates with the other stakeholder groups and can create a landslide in the overall level of support.[1] That is not to say that you should totally ignore the adversarial group of stakeholders; rather, be cognizant to the fact that we often focus on them rather than lead the fence-sitters.

---

[1]Michael Nir, *Project Management: Influence and Leadership Building Rapport in Teams, A practical guide* (Boston, MA: Sapir Publishing, 2014).

▨ **Anti-Pattern** Why do we focus on the adversary group? Psychologically speaking, we have a need to be accepted and loved (or at least liked), and we find it extremely difficult to be in a position where people are unaccepting of us. We go to great lengths to receive appreciation and support from groups of people who disagree with us and/or our goals.

In the first 90 days, I highly recommend building the base of support for the program by letting go of the explicit need for unanimous, all-encompassing acceptance. This isn't an easy task and requires a mental and cognitive shift in how we perceive ourselves and our interactions with the environment in which we operate. Achieving this improved psychological condition enables us to move away from focusing on those who aren't accepting us and instead investing time and effort in those who are supportive or those who haven't made up their mind yet.

> As a general rule of thumb, in any interaction that you might have, approximately 5% of the stakeholders will be against, 5% of the stakeholders will be in favor, and the remaining 90% of stakeholders will be either fence sitters or paying some amount of lip service.
>
> —Michael Nir[2]

Focus the efforts on the stakeholders who support the vision and promote it with those who are still wavering, the fence sitters. Share the success stories with the entire organization, yet avoid investing time and effort by trying to convince opposing stakeholders.

Consider a Silicon Valley-based integrated circuit engineering and manufacturing company that was facing a prominent decline in market share due to changing usage patterns among consumers. The leadership embraced the lean unifying framework, articulated a vision, and participated in the executive training. While support for the program was in place among marketing, finance, and software engineering, I identified resistance with the hardware engineering, operations, and regional sales business units. The deeper analysis did confirm that the senior vice presidents of the opposing business units viewed the program suspiciously; some were more in line with the vision than others. Building on the CEO's support for the program, I enlisted a high-profile program team to act on the ideas that emerged from the executive workshop. The cross-functional team had members of the supporting business units as well as some members of the adversarial business units. I had to work with

---

[2]Michael Nir, *Project Influence and Leadership: Building Rapport in Teams*, 5th ed. (Boston, MA: Sapir Consulting Publishing, 2013).

this team in the first 90 days to identify customer personas, prototype an MVP, and run experiments with customers to validate their hypotheses.

Since at this point a few of the senior vice presidents opposing the program were taking a passive role, I saw the opportunity to find members of their organization that were supporting the effort. This required me to continue identifying support for the vision as I was learning the realities of the business. I used the learning to persuade mid-level managers in the business units of the adversarial senior vice presidents to support the program. The five cross-functional teams that emerged from the first executive training had a mix of supporters and a few fence sitters. By the completion of the 90-day program and the demonstration of successful results, I had gained momentum and sufficient buy-in to proceed to the next phase.

I often expect two or three of the five first MVPs identified in the exectuive workshop to exhibit benefits at the 90-day mark. This is in line with lean thinking; you must assume that there will be a pivot and you need to clearly communicate it throughout the 90 days. Failure by validation is welcome, and it is part of learning. However, failing to communicate that you expect some of the programs to pivot will lead prominent adversarial business leaders to call the program itself a failure. **Protect the program by promoting the concept of learning by failure; share the expectation that not all ideas will yield beneficial results, and yet the lean engine enables much faster turnaround time in learning which ideas do not have merit.** Figure 8-1 is a graphical representation that carries this message: We expect ideas to fail; the failure is a result of continuous validation following the scientific method.

Figure 8-1. Many ideas exist and our goal is to provide a framework to quickly test and pivot or persevere. (Source: Graphic design by Hen Nir. © Sapir Consulting US LLC 2017, www.michaelnir.com)

▦ **Best Practice** The first teams emerging from the executive training self-select projects on which they will implement the lean approach. I prefer that they select project/product/feature/opportunities; however, I rarely limit them and often this can result in non-product related ideas. Thus, leaders identify huge undertakings that the organization has been struggling with for some time. The art and skill of this step is to identify a meaningful MVP that can be validated in 90 days and create a marked impact on the business. When non-product ideas are selected, the resulting 90-day MVP might be the validation of the removal of non-necessary process steps, which in itself is a win.

Identify Customer Personas

More effort is required during the first 90 days in developing personas. Let's revisit what you learned previously: in many organizations, personas are treated as a sign of being "modern." Pictures are laminated on the wall and persona stories are included in employee booklets. However, personas should be as living and breathing as the people who they represent. Creating static types of your users and customers is counterproductive because it represents a point in time rather than allowing the persona to evolve with your thinking. Thus, consider personas as continuously evolving, much as the customer persona evolves along with a company's understanding of the target audience and their needs.

Anti-Pattern I view the lofty laminated persona pictures and associated details on the walls as you enter the main offices of a corporation as another case of bad smell. For me it is a sign of misinterpretation of the concept. When persona creation is a onetime effort usually led by user interface and user experience experts, the results are a superficial understanding of the consumer.

I discussed inside-out thinking, which is prevalent in many organizations and in many industries; moving to outside-in thinking is the focus of the first 30 days, which is then followed with actual interaction with consumers in the 90-days timeframe to jumpstart the creation of the personas. It is true that insight into the personas is also based on data, research, and surveying; however, in the true spirit of gemba, nothing substitutes direct interaction with real consumers.

Go see; ask why; show respect.

—Fujio Cho, Toyota chairman

Treat the creation of a persona as a learning process in itself. Follow up with the five cross-functional teams that completed the training and coach them to validate their assumptions about the persona they drafted during the executive training. A recurring pattern is that the organizations are often convinced that their assumptions about their consumers are true; however, once researched, many of these assumptions prove to be false.

As mentioned, big organizations and corporations are frequently characterized by little interaction with customers both internal and external. Use the first 90 days to challenge the prevailing organizational mindset that "we aren't allowed to interact with consumers." Ask the teams to clearly state the assumption about the draft persona and **push back on their inclination to use existing internal data to validate it**. Rather, request that they validate their assumptions by interacting directly with real people outside the offices, in the real world. For executive teams that hardly ever interact with a consumer, this is a quite a challenge. They usually bring up various legal and compliance excuses to push back; however, this is just a smokescreen masking their fear of actually going out of the building and validating their assumptions. When I tasked executive teams with validating their assumptions concerning the personas they created with real consumers, they often hid behind surveys and regulations.

Anti-Pattern Teams in organizations that rarely reach out to their consumers tend to blame it on various legal and regulatory restrictions. While some may be true, most of the excuses are actually a disguise for an innate fear of reaching out to consumers and getting unfiltered feedback about the products and services. This fear is evident and possibly justified in legacy industries where consumers are captured audiences.

The goal of the first 90 days is to break the fear and empower the teams to validate their assumptions concerning the draft persona they created. This is an initial step in the creation of a *living* persona. I will revisit the topic in the next chapter.

A persona can be summed in a simple graphic design, as shown in Figure 8-2. Avoid a pretty image of the person; sketch roughly instead.

Figure 8-2. A graphic captures the main attributes, experiences, thoughts, and feelings of the persona. (Source: Graphic design by Hen Nir. © Sapir Consulting US LLC 2017, www.michaelnir.com)

Tip What if the consumer is an internal customer? Some of the ideas stemming from the training sessions will eventually lead to creating an internal persona. That's fine; in many organizations employees in one business unit are oblivious to the impacts of their decisions on a downstream business unit. Therefore identifying a persona for an internal customer makes sense and is useful in clarifying any assumptions concerning them.

The best example of the gap between the laminated, colorful, synthetic persona exhibited on the corporate office walls and the real, flesh-and-blood consumer occurred in the offices of a private health insurance provider in London. The laminated persona was a smiling, 60-year-old city dweller who was engaged in sports and the community, led a healthy life, and yet suffered from a certain chronic disease. There were numerous details concerning his lifestyle, dwelling, fears, and concerns. However, the persona didn't convey the true essence of the consumer; rather it conveyed a cheerful disposition. When I conducted a user-centered design workshop with the executive team working through their persona assumptions, a different and starker persona appeared, one that allowed a much deeper appreciation of who the consumer was. It was similar to upgrading from a flat two-dimensional view to a three-dimensional view. The wall-mounted persona models could not capture the key feeling and experiences of the persona and thus contributed to a skewed perception of the possible solution.

Tip   Remember the microwave example from the introduction? What if you created a rudimentary cardboard prototype of a microwave and used it at a local mall to interact with an unfiltered, non-persona-specific population. What might you learn?

Prototype MVP and Program Training

The training program that commenced with the executive team proceeds with training targeted to mid-level management. The goal of the first 90 days is to have approximately 3-5% of the employees trained. Considering a reasonably sized enterprise of 10,000 to 20,000 employees, this translates to roughly 500 to 1,000 mid-level managers trained. Each class holds about 25 participants grouped in five predefined cross-functional teams of five individuals each. On average, you can expect to run several dozens of these classes.

Best Practice   Does this mean that you should embark on a hiring spree before you roll out the program? Not necessarily. I found that the members of the PMO, Scrum Masters, UX experts, and others in various backgrounds that have the right mindset serve well as trainers and coaches to the program, in addition to targeted hiring for trainers.

By the end of the first month, you should have identified and trained internal regional trainers to facilitate the program. Each of these trainers will then become a mentor and coach for the teams they train, supporting them weekly in getting them prepared for their separate 90-day demonstrations. I suggest that you schedule demonstrations regionally with members of the executive leadership participating in person to review the results of the MVP validations.

The training program follows the same approach described in the previous chapter:

- Pre-workshop individual assignments
- Workshop: Two-day, hands-on, experiential workshop
- Workshop first evening reflection
- Workshop team assignment
- Team post-workshop activity
- Team lean startup coaching
- Team exhibition

Each trainer-made coach supports up to six classes worth of participants, thus they need to be fully engaged and committed to the program. The weekly coaching session are scheduled for 30 minutes, hence about half their time is committed to these sessions.

Tip I was hesitant whether to present the full program details for the enterprise, since it might instill some concern with readers who do not command the organizational resources to set a plan such as this in motion. However, I wanted to detail a comprehensive approach to enterprise success; I have implemented smaller scale efforts with much success. Actually, you could start with 6 teams, 4 or even a single team to validate assuumptions and demostrate the results!

The MVPs are defined by each team during the training; the goal of each team is to identify the assumption that will be validated by the MVP. That's challenging because the team is unsure what the MVP should look like. Often the first coaching sessions are spent refining the MVP and brainstorming which assumptions must be validated.

As part of creating the MVP, the teams identify facts and assumptions. They use Post-It notes to capture facts separately, and they follow the same process to identify assumptions. They share the assumptions and remove redundancies. Often what seems like a fact is actually an assumption. Figure 8-3 captures two facts on two separate Post-It notes. On closer scrutiny, we revised our fact concerning the blue worm. We don't know for sure whether Ross, our persona, would eat a blue worm.

Figure 8-3. Facts and assumption about the persona emerge from the MVP. (Source: Graphic design by Hen Nir. © Sapir Consulting US LLC 2017, www.michaelnir.com)

The important/uncertain grid that follows is introduced in the training as a tool to identify the most important and the most uncertain assumptions that are embedded within the MVP and the persona. An example of the important/ uncertain grid is presented in Figure 8-4. The team maps the assumptions into the grid individually and then discusses the discrepancies together.

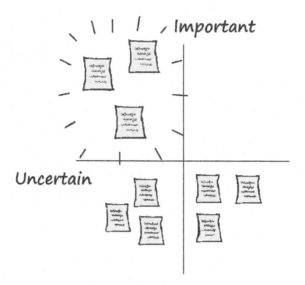

Figure 8-4. The facts and assumption grid (Source: Graphic design by Hen Nir.
© Sapir Consulting US LLC 2017, www.michaelnir.com)

▦ **Tip**   Do teams self-select ideas for projects or are those driven by the executive team's ideas?
I struggled with this question for quite some time. There are benefits for both approaches. On the
one hand, allowing the teams self-select ideas for projects conveys a message of empowerment:
you are giving the employees control of their destiny, you are sending a clear message that you
welcome their contribution to the vision, and you trust them to come up with the ideas that would
make the most sense for them. On the other hand, you expose yourself to the danger of having
ideas that don't really impact the organization from the perspective of the overarching vision and
some of the ideas are mediocre. I have seen both occur and yet most often stayed the course
of allowing each team a control of its own destiny, assuming that top-down controlled planning
of ideas would not necessarily lead to better results. I'll let you be the judge and decider on how to
approach the topic.

Run Experiments with Customers to Validate Your Hypotheses

The sense of urgency is on; you must run experiments with your consumers
to validate the assumptions that the teams identified. There is little that
stands in your way to accomplish this, apart from the resistance that the
teams themselves exhibit. The fear of getting out of the comfort zone and
asking for direct feedback on their ideas, assumptions, and hypotheses is not

something they were ever training to perform. The best method to overcome this resistance is to coach the teams, post the two-day training, to start experimenting with the customer immediately without letting the fear sink in. The learnings from the simplest of experimentation are vast. The teams I coach often discover that they crafted the wrong hypotheses or that the hypotheses were quickly refuted. Once they start, they get excited since they are receiving unfiltered feedback to their idea, something that for most is a revelation.

■ **Tip**   The unfiltered learning that occurs at this phase in the first 90 days is nothing short of mind-blowing. The ideas that the executive team selects and are validated shortly provide initial answers to long-time questions that the enterprise has been implicitly struggling with. Make sure you capture the discoveries and share them with the wider organization to grow the support for the program.

I already shared the following figure; I will use it again to further explain the validation process. You completed the training with each team having several assumptions (that are important or uncertain) to validate. Figure 8-5 describes the overall process. I will detail the steps starting with Hypothesize through Pivot.

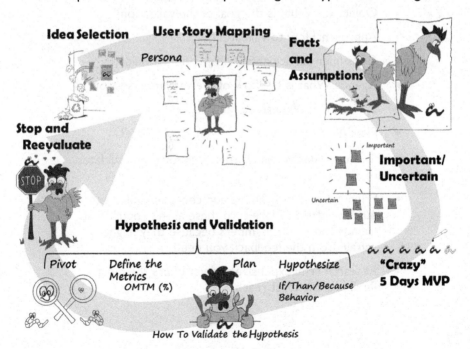

Figure 8-5. Lean startup workshop (validation planning) (Source: Graphic design by Hen Nir. © Sapir Consulting US LLC 2017, www.michaelnir.com)

The Lean Engine Description

The steps described in Figure 8-5 are the following:

- **Hypothesize**: As early as the first day of the workshop, explain the importance of clearly stating a hypothesis. By the second day, the participants are prepped to think about the assumption they have concerning their idea in the context of a hypothesis. The difference between an assumption and a hypothesis is the measurability. *We might assume that chickens will eat blue worms. However, the hypothesis is numerical and measurable: **if** we offer 10 chickens four dietary options, **then** at least 5 of them will eat the blue worm **because** they agree with this type of food.*

- **Plan**: How are you validating the hypothesis? Who will you engage? How would you find them? What would you need for that? The plan answers these questions and more. *We recruited Ross and gave him a light blue bib and silverware. We placed a blue worm in front of him to observe his dietary preferences.*

- A full plan will discuss the following:

  - Objectives: What is the goal of the validation?

  - Approach: How to validate?

  - Consumer participants: With whom to validate?

  - Agenda: What is the flow of the validation session?

  - Environment: Where to validate?

  - Plan: What is the overall timeline to validate?

- Part of the validation plan is to search for the candidates. There are various sources:

  - Friends and family: Simple and cheap for initial and quick validation. Make sure these aren't you closest friends and family members because they might refrain from the feedback you need.

  - Research firm: Expensive and yet offers the most flexible and widest reach.

- Social media: Effective and rather cheap. Allows a medium reach, although it requires a network to operate on.

- Ad hoc: When you need really fast responses to short questions, you can validate at your office, the next-door company, the mall, or your favorite coffee shop. That's exactly what gemba is all about.

- There are various methods to quickly mock up and prototype an MVP without investing in any upfront software or hardware development. Consider the following:

  - Concierge MVP: Identify valuable MVP elements and perform them manually.

  - Wizard of Oz: Behind the curtain you operate the functions either manually or via existing product and technology.

  - Dry Wallet: Measure price point, for example, by offering a dummy "purchase now" option.

  - Video: Video of "real life" scenario to validate interest.

  - Crowdsourcing: Similar to dry wallet; however it's a faster, anonymous roll out to validate interest.

- Define the metrics: At the same time that you plan for the validation, you identify the metrics you will use to assess the results of the validation. It is true that you initially discuss the metrics as you craft the hypothesis; however, you often need to break it down and further detail it. I introduced the concept of vanity metrics in Chapter 5. You need to identify metrics that matter. I also differentiated between output-outcome-impact metrics. Effective MVP validation is done by focusing on outcome and impact metrics. *What if Ross doesn't peck the worm? Is this a success?*

- More on metrics…

  - The One Metric That Matters (OMTM) is a metric that

    - Provides a clear answer to your questions

    - Drives focus on the objective

    - Speeds the build-measure-learn cycle

- An effective metric is

  - A ratio rather than an absolute number (new sales per hour)

  - Simple, such as *revenue per time unit or product*

  - Comparative, relevant for A/B testing

- Metrics evolve through the program. The metrics for validating a problem are different than the metrics for validating a solution and for validating a MVP and ongoing feature hypothesis validation. While the former are measured qualitatively and often done through interviewing, the latter are measured quantitatively and are described as profit or savings ratios.

■ **Tip**   Following the microwave example, what would the elements of a plan to validate look like?

Pivot or Persevere in a Build-Measure-Learn Cycle

A few pivots occur in the first 90 days, and you need to support the process of learning and failing. As mentioned, a pivot is a result of a hypothesis being invalidated, which means that the original assumption was wrong. The failing part is difficult to accept, especially if the assumption has been one that the organization believed in for a long time. Additionally, for members of the executive team, accepting that they were wrong is sometimes difficult to acknowledge.

■ **Best Practice**   An assumption can be broken down into one or more hypotheses. In case of an assumption being broken into many hypotheses, make sure you aren't claiming the whole assumption is wrong when only a subset of its hypotheses were invalidated.

Framing the failure as part of an ongoing **build-measure-learn** cycle assists in accepting the failure as part of the learning. This cycle is at the heart of lean thinking in the enterprise. The build-measure-learn cycle questions the concept of "big bang" deliveries, which dominated development and project management for a long time. Big bang approaches became prevalent in the past as organizations grew in size and distanced themselves from consumers, products increased in complexity, mass production and mass marketing ruled, and assembly lines spanned continents. We lost sight of the need to build, get feedback from customers by measuring, learning, and then iterating based on the learning. The agile software movement that officially started with the Agile Manifesto in 2001 was a catalyst towards iterative development. It was both a driver and a response to the market demand for product personalization, getting software products to market faster, and aligning the product to the actual needs of the consumer. There is some criticism about the fast iterative feedback approach in the sense that it prohibits monumental undertakings and limits the development to small improvements.[3] However, the criticism doesn't answer the problems of the remarkable waste occurring in the creation of results.

Figure 8-6 illustrates the concept of a pivot resulting from a build-measure-learn cycle. The build process has to be as small as possible, hence the concepts of MVP; the measurement has to measure the outcome. Notice that in this case, Ross the rooster didn't ask for a progress report of *twigs per square foot* from the IT department or for a status report of *hours invested to build the nest* from Operations. He measures an outcome by interacting with the actual build; he sits in the MVP nest to validate fit-for-use. Unfortunately, the hypothesis is invalidated and the MVP assumption fails. Ross falls down. Was a safety cushion provided for him to fall into? When implementing a build-measure-learn cycle, you need to make sure you address the **safety nets protecting the company in case of failures**. Part of the first 90 days is learning and putting in place such safety nets.

[3]For example, Peter Thiel and Blake Masters, *Zero to One: Notes on Startups, or How to Build the Future* (New York, NY: Currency, 2014).

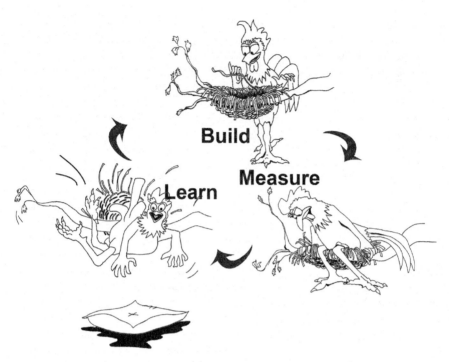

Figure 8-6. Build-measure-learn cycle (pivot) (Source: Graphic design by Hen Nir. © Sapir Consulting US LLC 2017, www.michaelnir.com)

▨ **Best Practice** Address the issue of safety nets early on. Identify and formulize the required mechanisms that allow the safety of failure and communicate broadly, so employees aren't surprised. Communicate that failure is an option.

What happens when there are no safety nets in place? Consider a financial services enterprise that adopted lean thinking to speed the integration and deployment of a back-end core system to replace an obsolete legacy system. It was a revolutionary approach because it focused on an **internal core system**. Traditionally, replacements of legacy systems and deployment of new IT core systems are lengthy projects, often costly, and normally under deliver on the promised results.

The team was using the build-measure-learn cycle to cut down the requirements gathering process, remove exceptions, and speed the time to deploy. They identified an MVP for a new product and created the required mechanisms to support the purchase, use, and support capabilities on the new system. They spent several months constructing the minimal core functionalities. Prior to the launch, they met with the various business owners and asked them for the possible impacts of various scenarios. The operations team and the manager of the consumer representative organization estimated that the impacts of the MVP would be minimal. No special plans were put in place in case things went wrong. Based on this, they decided to roll out the new MVP functionality across all of the lower 48 states (US).

The day after launch, vital signs showed a small increase in waiting times at the call centers. Two days later, the waiting times were doubled. By day three, the average wait time for a customer representative quadrupled. It was less than a week before urgent meetings started to appear on calendars. Executives were called in, the program was halted, and fall-back scenarios discussed. As is the case in enterprises, finger pointing started and blame was assigned. It didn't matter that the senior vice president of operations estimated small impact prior to the go-live. Now his business unit was paying for the additional hours and days of work, and he was outraged. The program lost credibility and the term "MVP" was ridiculed. At this point, they decided to roll back the deployment and deploy the solution state by state, which is a fundamental concept of MVP deployment. On top of which no safety nets were in place.

■ **Tip** Discuss the various options for the MVP from a business perspective; there are many degrees of freedom to limit the impact of validating gone wrong. Always communicate your intentions.

The hypothesis can also be validated, in which case the company perseveres. It proceeds with the next most important and most uncertain assumption, validating the relevant hypothesis. Figure 8-7 illustrates the concept of persevering in a build-measure-learn cycle. The build process has to be as small as possible, hence the concept of MVP. The metrics must measure the outcome. Notice again that Ross the rooster didn't ask for a forecast *development effort* from the enterprise PMO. By interacting with the actual build he measures an outcome; he sits in the MVP nest to validate fit-for-use. Ross then learns about the building process. Is the nest comfortable? Is it safe? Can it support his weight for a period of time?

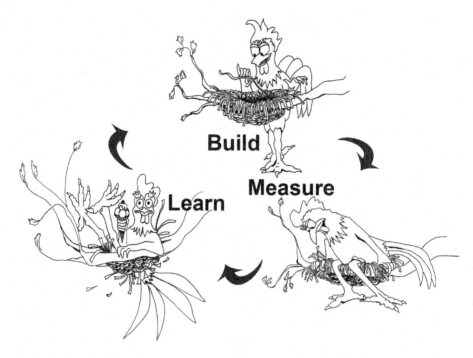

Figure 8-7. Build-measure-learn cycle (persevere) (Source: Graphic design by Hen Nir. © Sapir Consulting US LLC 2017, www.michaelnir.com)

He is ready to experiment with the next step. He will validate another hypothesis; each complete loop through the cycle either adds to the MVP or redirects it. The solution will emerge through an ongoing repeat of the build-measure-learn cycle.

■ **Tip** What might be the various business options to limit the MVP in your organization?

First 12 Months

Executing, Mentoring, and Reviewing

It has been 12 months since you started. What should your daily schedule look like? What should you emphasize?

The first year flew by. As you'll read in section three, the first 12 months of any transformation are intense and rewarding, filled with success and failure. Table 9-1 details the expected percentage of time allocated around the yearly anniversary of the transformation.

***Table 9-1.** Expected Percentage of Time Allocated–First 12 Months*

Activity	Time Spent	Comments
Define vision	10%	Revisit the vision
Identify customer personas	15%	Ongoing
Prototype MVP and program training	15%	From MVP to MMR and ongoing community of practice (CoP) coaching
Run experiments	40%	Experiment locally, collect data quickly, and decide fast
Pivot or persevere	20%	Continue supporting the program

© Michael Nir 2018
M. Nir, *The Pragmatist's Guide to Corporate Lean Strategy*,
https://doi.org/10.1007/978-1-4842-3537-9_9

Revisit Vision

A year since you started with the lean agile transformation is the appropriate occasion to revisit the vision with the executive team, possibly at the yearly offsite. I often facilitate the discussion as a retrospective, using the postcard from the future that we constructed the previous year as a reference point. Figure 7-1 from Chapter 7 presented a compelling vision for my client; after a year they were ready to review their vision, update, and adapt it. They answered questions such as

- Why are we on this journey?

- What have we learned as an organization?

- What are our main lessons from the last year?

- What could we have done differently?

- Is our original vision still relevant? Do we need to change it? Do we need to update it?

- What do we want to start doing to support the updated vision?

- What would our new postcard from the future look like?

I facilitate these sessions with the leadership team as well as in town halls to get the necessary buy-in to proceed with the program.

Stakeholder management, which was a prevalent activity in the first 90 days, is still a priority, however of less intensity. The critical mass of support is achieved within the first six to nine months; the fence sitters are convinced by this time and join the supporter stakeholder team. This is a result of the ongoing success of the program.

What do you do if you don't have the support you need by the end of the first year?

Sometimes, the lean agile program is grassroots and locally grown, and it's difficult to take it to the next level in the enterprise. This isn't the intention when you roll it out since it is always the best to receive the support from the top and have the executive buy-in needed when starting the program; however, you can't always have it. This is normally the case when there is local sponsorship but a lack of interest in the enterprise to support it. By the end of the 12 months, you have an indication of whether you can receive the necessary funding to roll out the program across a bigger part of the organization. I suggest building the case for this expansion by evangelizing the successes achieved on the local level to executives in other parts of the business. Many times people have their heads down, creating great results in one part of the business, and assume that their success is widely known.

More often than not, this isn't the case in big enterprises. The great results affect a business unit of 500 employees and could be limited to a geographical location. The employees creating these results are too busy working miracles and thus the task of communicating the evolving vision is left to you, the lean agile transformation expert. I observe it as an extended part of stakeholder management; it isn't the traditional limited approach that you'll read about. It is up to you to take the results and popularize them across the enterprise to find those interested in supporting you.

■ **Anti-Pattern**   Bad smell: Actually, many times I've observed various transformations occurring at an enterprise of 15,000 employees; all have their merits but they aren't a holistic approach.

I've been in these situations several times; we were able to create powerful results both lean and agile. I was convinced that others in the bigger enterprise were aware of our success, but that wasn't the case. When I met by chance an executive at a trade show and we had lunch together, I was surprised that she knew little of our achievements. Actually she was looking for a similar program and didn't know who to turn to. I've learned since not to take it for granted, in bigger enterprises, when the lean agile transformation is limited to a business unit. By the time we have our first wins, we make sure we communicate them to the bigger organization. Often we'll run into others who are interested in doing the same, and we'll happily support them in their journey. Other times we'll meet more opposition and we'll figure out how to lead through it. Most likely that other business unit has an invested interest in another approach or method, and is reluctant to invest in another, or maybe they tried some of these ideas and they didn't quite work for them. That's often the case with failed lean agile efforts: trying a limited subset with little support, and when failing, declaring the system faulty rather than the lopsided implementation. In these cases, I suggest looking beyond what people are saying to what they are doing. Looking for the commonalities and finding possible areas of mutual interest is a reliable method to grow the lean agile approach outside the original area of implementation.

■ **Tip**   When you are in position to affect approaches being driven in various parts of the enterprise, ALWAYS evangelize the similarities and identify a single consistent model, as I described several times in this book.

As I describe in section three, by the end of the first year, the program succeeds in creating the critical mass in supporting the new way of work. However, where did the employees find the bandwidth to complete the initial lean pilots that occured throughout the first 12 months? When I initially introduced the model described in Chapter 7 at a client of mine, we asked ourselves who would be the people to drive the change, the new way of work. We found two answers, both presented in books.

John Kotter is a thought leader in the fields of business, leadership, and change. His 1996 best-selling book on leading change in organizations is widely referenced and still holds true in 2018, specifically the eight steps to a successful transformation. In the enterprises where we didn't have allocated resources to the program, *XLR8*,[1] Kotter's follow-on work from 2014 describes an approach we used to model our lean agile transformation in the first 12 months. In *XLR8*, Kotter argues that established legacy organizational structures do not provide the agility to respond quickly to narrow windows of opportunity. Kotter suggests the organizations augment their hierarchical top-down structure with a loose startup like a distributed network built from individuals representing various domains in the enterprise. In essence, he suggests a dual-operating system with the hierarchical top-down legacy structure providing day-to-day management and the network providing necessary responses to the opportunities. Kotter is convinced that this network existed in most enterprises at a much earlier stage of their evolution. This belief is shared by Eric Ries and is described in *The Startup Way*.

Kotter's vision inspired ours both in application and strategy. It provided the visionary support we needed from a prominent figure in change leadership that is not part of the lean agile movement. It was an outside-in affirmation to business agility thinking that we implemented. It also proposed and validated the mechanism to successfully transform an organization that was at capacity in terms of resource allocation.

Another inspiration for the vision was found in *The 4 Disciplines of Execution*.[2] The book offers an additional outside-in view on creating change in resource-constrained organizations. It describes the endless daily tasks that employees handle as the *whirlwind*; rather than battle it, they suggest accepting it as a necessary evil in maintaining the current organization. The whirlwind is the massive amount of energy that's necessary just to keep the operation going on a day-to-day basis. At the same time, it provides a framework to implement WIGS (widely important goals). The 4 disciplines aren't designed for managing your whirlwind but for executing your most critical strategy in the midst of your whirlwind. We used the 4 disciplines to lead the lean agile change

---

[1] John P. Kotter; *Accelerate: Building Strategic Agility for a Faster-Moving World*, (Watertown, MA: Harvard Business Review Press, 2014).
[2] Chris McChesney, Sean Covey, and Jim Huling, *The 4 Disciplines of Execution: Achieving Your Wildly Important Goals* (New York, NY: Free Press, 2016).

in several organizations that had no agile background. They are similar in thought and are more relevant in non-software environments.

■ **Best Practice**   *The Four Disciplines of Execution* and Kotter's *XLR8* provide inspiration in organizations where agility isn't widespread and where business rather than IT or software is prominent.

Identify Customer Personas

I haven't discussed the broader concepts of user experience (UX) and user experience strategy in this book, while I referred to it occasionally. Although not part of persona identification, various Lean UX concepts have been addressed over the 12 months. Jamie Levy[3] describes how to devise innovative digital products that people want. Since many of the steps to validate hypothesis involve interaction with internal and external customers, I recommend reading it to better understand how to define and validate the target users through provisional personas and customer discovery techniques, focus the team by running structured experiments using prototypes, and increase customer engagement by mapping desired user actions to meaningful metrics.

Organizations with low UX maturity require support in maturing their user experience strategy and implementation. Often, organizations do employ user experience experts; however, they are isolated from the main delivery effort and produce insights that are hard to incorporate into the products and features. What you'll find in the first 12 months is that user experience as a concept has to become second nature to everyone's' thinking; otherwise you'll end up with a microwave with too many buttons, a back office system that is annoying to use, a college curriculum that is outdated, or two pipes of one line that are supposed to meet yet are 2 feet apart when the welder tries to connect them.

■ **Best Practice**   Make user experience common knowledge, and facilitate user-centric design workshops as part of the training curriculum.

---

[3]Jamie Levy; *UX Strategy: How to Devise Innovative Digital Products that People Want* (Hoboken, NJ: O'Reilly Media, 2015).

Each pilot team will need user experience know-how early on. Make sure you're able to provide it to enable validation of hypothesis. Whether the organization is immature or mature, at approximately six months into the program and no later than 12 months, you'll need to unify the team level efforts. Revisit the personas that were identified. Most likely, if the teams had enough freedom to experiment, there are multiple personas in place; without an overarching strategy, many of them will be redundant. As long as the personas are created organically within teams that then validate assumptions about them, rather than centrally driven by an innovation lab and thorough research, you are on the right path. You have to strike a balance between the separate personas that the teams identified and the need for a cohesive approach for persona creation and validation. Make sure you communicate the personas in place and cross-share the understanding behind the various personas and their goals. I found it useful to aggregate personas into an arch type and made the distinction between the children and the parent arch type persona. Yet again, this is a balance, a tradeoff between letting each team ideate and explore, and a more robust centric approach. I prefer to err on giving more freedom to the team. Yes, you can and probably should design and provide the following to the teams as optional resources:[4]

- Unified surveys reports
- Survey templates
- Interview scripts
- Sample questions for stakeholders
- Analysis report formats
- Customer profiles
- Recruitment participants criteria check lists
- Recruitment screening guidelines
- Design templates
- Facilitator/observer note-taking sheets

Be wary, though, of overburdening the teams with them and be open to experimentation with the resources you provide the team members. **Being lean agile is also being open to adapt the process and change it as needed.**

---

[4]These and others can be found here: *User Experience Research Templates and Examples*, Office of Energy Efficiency and Renewable Energy, www.energy.gov/eere/communicationstandards/user-experience-research-templates-and-examples.

■ **Best Practice**   Business agility is being able to question the process itself rather than following blindly the prescriptive processes and procedures that were created by our predecessors.

Prototype MVP

There is often confusion when discussing the term *minimal valuable product* (MVP). When the teams start out, they often refer to MVP in its true sense; MVP constitutes a subset of a new feature or product which the team believes they can validate with the customer, internal or external. It is used to cheaply experiment and answer a hypothesis. The goal is validated learning. The team uses it to figure out what the customer is interested in. The MVP might not be actualized using code or software. Through a series of MVP experiments the team might build an minimal marketable feature (MMF), which is the smallest set of features or subset of a product that is delivered. It has both value to the organization and the customer, internal or external. The series of MVP experiments might never culminate in an MMF as the team might pivot completely from the idea rather than persevere.

Following several releases of MMFs–or in other words, as the product is incrementally deployed–a major deployment might be considered a release, which is often termed a minimal marketable release (MMR). The goal of the team is to identify the smallest set of incrementally delivered features between releases that have value to the customer. Sometimes we refer to the term minimal marketable product (MMP), which is used to distinguish between an MMR that is targeted at a broader audience and an MMP that is aimed at initial users, typically innovators and early adopters. The team can use the MMP as a tool to reduce time to market by offering a limited subset of features.

■ **Tip**   Make sure people distinguish between an MVP and a MMF; never release an MVP to a broad audience.

When the teams form and work on the 90-day demo, they are invested in validating assumptions towards an MVP. At the executive demo that follows the 90 days, the presentation exhibits either failed experiments of MVPs or successful experiments that support an MVP; both provide validated learning! During the demonstration, the executive team discusses the merits of the successful validated MVPs. They decide together with the team what the next steps are. Often the team proceeds to validate the next assumption towards another MVP, and incrementally creates the MMF. Since the transition is incremental, it is tricky to define exactly when an MVP becomes an MMF and which MMF is actually an MMR, which is the reason they are often used interchangeably. However, confusing the names is detrimental since it results in too big MVPs, which leads to upfront development efforts that are too big and wasteful.

▓ **Anti-Pattern**   Bad smell: By calling everything an MVP, organizations are missing the point. They are investing too much upfront effort in validating big chunks rather than focusing on small minimal assumptions and building the product incrementally.

Expect the teams in training sessions to fall into this trap. They think of a big initiative and then quickly jump to the solution. They fall in love with the solution rather than the problem. Thinking of the solution will lead them to identify a big MVP that requires a major effort and they then **immediately claim that the project is irrelevant since they will never receive the necessary funding and resources to run the experiment**. It is a vicious cycle. Initial MVPs are small—small enough that a team of five can validate quickly—in no more than 30 days. Subsequent MVPs might require limited code and take longer to validate. If you start with a big MVP, you are wasting time and effort.

▓ **Best Practice**   As a coach, ask teams members how they can validate the MVP without any software code written and no automation provided!

One way to avoid the big MVP mistake by the team is ask them to identify the MVP by starting with a clean slate. As mentioned in Chapter 7, use user story mapping to identify the full breadth of a process from the perspective of a customer. Following Jeff Patton's *User Story Mapping*,[5] the team creates the user story map and then identifies a goal for a persona, a possible MVP. The MVP is a slice used to identify a small version of the feature or product. Team members identify the goal of the slice in a sticky note or card to the left of the story map. The next step most teams follow is removing steps from the process map to identify the smallest number of tasks that allow the specific persona to reach its goal. However, the net effect is that too many process steps remain on the map. In other words, removing process steps leads to more work to be completed compared with starting from a clean slate. I ask

---

[5]Jeff Patton, *User Story Mapping: Discover the Whole Story, Build the Right Product*, (Hoboken, NJ: O'Reilly Media, 2014).

team members to first remove all the process steps from the map, and only then add back the steps that are absolutely necessary for the MVP slice. **By starting from a clean slate a much smaller MVP emerges.**

■ **Tip** When we are tasked with remove elements, psychological loss aversion kicks in and we find it difficult to let go; when we start with a clean slate, the discussion is free from the loss aversion bias.

You will also find that those trained in project management who are familiar with the Work Breakdown Structure concept and tool find it hard to embrace MVP concepts. They treat the customer journey as a project and break down the project into elements, thus creating big chunks of work. Instead, explain that user story maps are built grassroots without knowing the full scope of the projects, since the project and the scope change as they creating MVPs and validate assumptions to support them or pivot from them.

I ran into the above MVP challenge with a financial services organization. They created so-called MVPs that were too large for the team to validate in a short timeframe. The MVPs were broken down from a traditional marketing requirement document. **Each set of requirements was defined as an MVP and was identified as a fact rather than an assumption.** This is a recurring pattern. Traditional scope documents do identify assumptions; however, they never receive any validation treatment. **The MVPs this organization created were just milestone deliveries in a long process of creating feature upon feature, which resulted in wasteful development and had little to do with the essence of an MVP.**

■ **Anti-Pattern** Bad smell: Most marketing and business requirement documents have assumptions listed on page 3 or 4 of the 120-page document. These assumptions are listed in the document and then treated as facts for the reminder of the project.

For each 10 teams trained you can realistically expect

- In the first three months, half the teams will validate an MVP that will catch the attention of the leadership team and receive funds to proceed with more validation.
- Half of those will be able to build on that MVP and create substantial impact through an MMR.
- Other teams will regroup and continue experimenting with more ideas.

- The lean agile engine will impact individuals across the organization, who will want to be part of the in group and test more assumptions and validate MVPs.

- Ongoing quarterly demonstrations of potential new features and products, with either pivot or persevere decisions based on validated learning.

How do you coach and sustain these results? Following the training session, each team receives weekly or biweekly coaching supporting it in validating assumptions. At some point, you'll have to train trainers and coach coaches to provide a bigger reach of the program and answer the incoming requests for training and coaching. The Chapter 10 case study illustrates well the repercussions of a limited bandwidth.

I implemented communities of practice to increase the reach of the program. According to *Cultivating Communities of Practice* by Wenger, McDermott, and Snyder,[6] a community of practice is a group of people who share a concern or a passion for something they do, and learn how to do it better as they interact regularly. This definition reflects the fundamentally social nature of human learning. In all cases, the key elements are

- **The domain**: Members are brought together by a learning need they share (whether this shared learning need is explicit or not and whether learning is the motivation for their coming together or a by-product of it).

- **The community**: Their collective learning becomes a bond among them over time (experienced in various ways and thus not a source of homogeneity).

- **The practice**: Their interactions produce resources that affect their practice (whether they engage in actual practice together or separately).

The communities revolved around the various domains we required to operate the lean agile teams effectively. Most important was the lean agile coaching community and the user experience validation community. We jump-started the process and then had individuals responsible for coordinating and facilitating the meetings, recording lessons learned, and supporting the community. The communities were open to all. We encouraged aspiring coaches to attend the coaches community of practice as much as we encouraged others to join the communities that were of most interest to them. We reviewed practices that

---

[6]Etienne Wenger, Richard McDermott, and M. William Snyder, *Cultivating Communities of Practice* (Watertown, MA: Harvard Business Review Press, 2002).

the community identified and spread them across other communities to be used as best practices. We knew we were successful when the process was self-sustained after the first 12 months of the program.

■ **Best Practice**   Communities of practice done well are a great tool to share and spread knowledge in a distributed environment.

Run Experiments with Customers to Validate Your Hypotheses

I found myself drawn to experimenting with customers in the lean agile implementations I led, so I guess I have a skewed perception as to the amount of time you'll find yourself investing in this activity. That said, experimenting with customers to validate the hypotheses is a challenging, fun, and illuminating activity that clients find intriguing and foreign to their day jobs. Traditionally this is a combined skillset activity: the experimenting is handled by user experience experts and experienced interviewers while the data analysis is the domain of data experts and statisticians. Setting up A/B tests, defining population and sample size, and inferring the results are complex skills. However, if you truly want a lean agile assumption validation mindset that guides decision making, you must popularize these skills. As a coach I spent many hours mentoring and coaching teams and individuals to break two recurring mental blocks: the first was that they were allowed to interact with customers and the second that basic statistics are not complex; to date I am not sure which block I found harder to face.

Instead of explaining why experimenting with customers to validate the hypotheses is a challenging, fun, and illuminating activity, I provide real world examples below. They are what you can expect throughout the first 12 months.

■ **Tip**   Experimenting with customers to validate hypotheses requires knowledge in user experience and statistics. Coach your teams and individuals to be comfortable with these skills.

One of my engagements with a corporate lean strategy engagement was at a health insurance organization. The executive training was completed and I was spending time with the vice president of operations to discuss the first 30 days of the engagement. We were examining the five executive teams' projects when a director of IT dropped by and asked for five minutes of her time. They invited me to stay in the room while he presented his problem. Three months prior, they concluded their Net Promoter Score survey, sent to 2 million customers. They received back 215,300 completed surveys, and out of them 13,128 surveys also had free text responses. They wanted to examine the free text responses to learn from their customers; however, they preferred to use software to analyze the free text rather than read each response separately, which seemed to make sense. They had an off-the-shelf software application to analyze the free text results and they fed it with a sample of the free text survey results. The software output was not valuable, or as he put it, it was garbage. It seemed that the off-the-shelf software wasn't targeted to this type of text analysis. In order to customize the software and teach it the specific tagging relevant for the survey data, they would have to invest several months of engineering effort. The IT director explained that they prepared a project plan for the necessary customization and they would like to present it to the change review board. He added that this important project would have to supersede existing high priority efforts that were currently in flight. He promised that once he got the approval, he would be able to provide an analysis of the free text responses in three months.

When the IT director left the room, I asked the VP to tell me more about the NPS survey and data. She gave me background information about the results and the importance of the program.

I asked her why they wanted to analyze the results. She answered, "To take action and resolve the most important recurring issues that arise from the written feedback analysis."

I asked her for the actual data.

Luckily she had a copy of it on a spreadsheet; all 13,128 surveys that had free text responses.

I asked her how many free text survey responses she and her fellow executives would need to read to identify the most important recurring issues that arose from the written feedback analysis.

She answered, "All of them."

I asked, "So you're willing to spend IT resources and three months' time to fully analyze all surveys, then convene the leadership team, and spend time reviewing the analysis, and then four months hence decide on an action plan to respond to the synthesized analysis, and maybe in a year you'll address the information that you have right here in front of you."

To which she said, "Well, we need to analyze them…"

She was right, of course. However, how many did she truly need to analyze?

"How about five?" I asked her. She was confused for a minute and then she responded incredulously, "What do you mean, just five?"

I asked her to pick five responses in random and review the free text field.

We learned that people think their premiums are too high and that costumer service is annoying. "No surprise there," she muttered.

I suggested we pick another survey randomly and review it. She obliged; another customer unhappy with the service.

"Let's select a seventh survey." She did. Another customer that thinks they are paying too much for the insurance. "No surprise there," she said. "I don't need the survey to know that," she added.

Best Practice   When you know nothing about a certain experience or event, a single data point will increase your knowledge about it infinitely from zero to one; the next data point will increase your knowledge 100%, from one to two. The third will increase it by 50%, from two to three data points. The fourth by 33% and so on… It's the law of diminishing returns that rules. Be careful. How much is enough and how much are you willing to pay for an additional data point? **Make your MVPs small to limit failure, experiment locally, collect data quickly, and decide fast.**

By the 20th random survey, a pattern emerged and a quick Pareto analysis told the story: 80% of the responses that were attributed to a single cause, premiums that were too high.

In 30 minutes, we reviewed 30 more surveys, reaching 50 surveys to validate our finding and found the same patterns. I asked, "What would the value be of reviewing 100 more, 1,000 more, or all of them?"

Needless to say, the urgent IT project to customize the analysis software was scrapped.

Tip   You often need a smaller sample than you think you need.

The prevalent mindset in organizations is: we need to be careful since the investment is big, and the impact is big, and we can't be wrong; we mustn't fail, therefore we need more data to decide, and then we'll ask for more data just to be sure.

Lean agile flips this mindset. Let's run a small experiment where the stakes are small, the investment is small, the impact is small, and if we fail, we learn; therefore we don't need too much data to decide.

■ **Tip**   When dealing with health and safety issues, you want very high levels of confidence before deciding whether a process, feature, or product is safe. In these cases, the sample size out of the population must be much higher than anything I mentioned in this chapter.

Allow me to repeat this important point: the challenge we have as lean agile coaches is that we are fighting ingrained beliefs about data and decision making; we're up against decades of **faulty organizational perception that more is better and more analysis will always get you better results.**

As lean agile coaches, we know better. We realize that small iterative delivery with real customer feedback provides better and faster results. In other words, if it takes an organization 13 months to release a feature while its competitor is able to figure out the first MVP in 2 months and then iterate on the MVP, releasing an MMF 2 months later and continuing to iterate until they have a considerable market share in 7 months, guess who will dominate the market. **If time is of the essence, quick small releases that are validated with customers are a much better approach to creating value quickly.**

"Incremental product delivery will never work in our highly regulated industry," is what I heard from the vice president of product in an insurance company. He continued by explaining that **they have to file each and every new product in every single state and even the smallest change in the product has to be reapproved by the regulator.**

"Thus, it makes much more sense to file for every possible product variant upfront since it takes six month on average to receive the approval of the regulator in the state." He added. "I can't validate with a customer and then add a feature based on the feedback and ask to tweak the product accordingly. I must have everything up front!"

"That's valid," I answered.

"Then your system doesn't apply to our products and our industry."

"Really?"

I asked him how he offers the product that was approved by the regulator to the customer.

"Well, since it is approved, we develop the back-end functionally and give the customer plenty to choose from," he said. "They love it. I am sure of it."

"Well, do they?"

I offered a small experiment. "Let's ask our customers what they think of the options."

"Great. What kind of a coach are you?" the vice president exclaimed. "Exactly what I need now: another survey, more development work, more resources to complete it…"

I said that I would run the experiment with 10 consumers that selected a product online in a certain timeframe, others that spent longer, and another group that abandoned the online product selection system half-way through the selection process.

He wasn't all too happy about it but played along. Before we concluded our meeting, he mumbled, "I don't know what you expect to learn from 10 consumers."

Well, you might guess how the story unfolds. Turns out that the consumers didn't want to be exposed to all the options that were approved by the regulator, they found scrolling through 11 pages of various options confusing, and they really wished they could select from a small number of options. This is known as the paradox of choice.[7]

On top of which, IT software engineers spent an inordinate amount of time and money building the functionality on the back-end system. Wouldn't it make more sense figuring out which of the plans get the most interest and offer them?

He wasn't convinced. "You're just trying to save IT spending. What you validated is of little consequence." He kept offering the customer all 121 product variants presented in 11 web pages with 11 products per page.

You might be quietly criticizing this VP of product development. However, this is a recurring pattern. Enterprises offer too many options to a too-big demographic and resist proven best practices that explicitly instruct them otherwise.

That's why I find validating with customer so much fun. You get to go in the trenches and break entrenched beliefs, although not every engagement is successful, as this VP of product exemplifies.

Tip Now wait a minute. Before you start judging this organization critically, would your organization do otherwise? Would it trust statistics and avoid looking at all the data points in order to **act fast on the feedback from the consumer**?

---

[7] Barry Schwartz, *The Paradox of Choice* (New York, NY: Harper Perennial, 2005).

Pivot or Persevere in a Build-Measure-Learn Cycle

During the first 12 months you will support teams in moving away from their original assumptions and pivot. As mentioned, pivoting is hard. It is an admission of implicit or explicit failure. The more invested a team is in a certain product, feature, or project, the more difficult it is to pivot from it. Your role in the first 12 months is to stand guard and urge teams to call a hypothesis or an MVP invalid and move on. Initially, we used the rule of three: a team could persevere three times with their original idea before pivoting. Often the team would be unwilling to throw out an idea that they brought up and they might question the validation plan, the specific experiment, the sample size, and the participants. We wanted teams to feel ownership of the process and allowed them to persevere and conduct more testing; therefore we allowed three rounds. We used it for instructional purposes, although in hindsight it might be too lenient. We then became ruthless, and although we got pushback from teams, I think it was for the best.

Best Practice   Pivot ruthlessly. If the validation plan is intact and the hypothesis is invalidated, PIVOT.

In another case, the team was successful with the validation of the initial hypothesis but it was stuck on how to persevere. In other words, they were able to validate their most important and most uncertain assumption, and therefore persevered. However, they were at a loss on how to persevere: what was the next assumption to turn into a hypothesis and validate?

I found this to be another recurring pattern. People have an amazing idea, they think of one BIG assumption, and they are able to construct a hypothesis and validate it without any code developed, using a simple prototype, but then they get stuck. They are convinced that they are all done and their idea is ready to be developed completely. It's like they crossed the bridge and they have been vindicated. "Aha!!" They say, "You asked us to use this process and we used it and we showed you it works, so now give us the software or IT or other resources to make it a reality."

"Not so fast," I reply. "You've completed the first step in a long journey; what is your next most important and most uncertain assumption?"

I often hear that they don't have any. What should they do?

As a lean agile coach I find inspiration in Eric Ries's[8] four questions:

- Does the customer know they have the problem we are trying to solve?
- Can we build a solution for the problem?
- Will the customer buy the solution?
- Will they buy it from us?

These four questions are paramount; they guide the stuck teams to develop their next assumption to validate.

■ **Tip**   People will say, if we just had *that* we would conquer the market, win the competition, etc. *That* is often the most important and most uncertain assumption to validate. It turns out, though, that they lack the next assumption to validate–the next *that*–and asking them the four questions broadens their perspective and they are able to brainstorm more assumptions to validate.

Other times you'll find that teams call an assumption true too soon. They only validated one hypothesis that stemmed from that assumption; however, there are usually multiple hypotheses mapped to a single assumption and every single one needs to be validated. Take, for example, my discussion with the VP of product. I said that I experimented with 10 consumers in three groups in order to disprove **his assumption** that consumers want many products. It was easy to disprove since I only needed a single hypothesis, something like "if I ask 10 consumers, 9 will say that they hate the current product offering."

■ **Tip**   You will find that it is quite easy to disprove assumptions and trickier to validate them, which is actually a good thing since it limits the upfront resource investment.

However, it doesn't inform us what the product offering should be; therefore, I might identify the following assumption:

Our customers want simple and limited selection to quickly choose a plan.

This is as vague as assumptions get, and similar to many that you'll run across; it is unclear what "simple" is, what "limited" means, and what "quickly" infers. The term "plan" itself is vague. Even the term "our customers" is ambiguous.

---

[8]Eric Ries, *The Lean Startup: How today's entrepreneurs use continuous innovation to create radically successful businesses* (New York, NY: Crown Business, 2011).

This assumption can be broken down to numerous hypotheses, each requiring its own validation plan. However, keep in mind that some of the hypothesis will be more important and uncertain than others. Some hypothesis you could solve by researching benchmarks, such as the time a customer is willing to spend selecting an insurance plan or a metric for a limited selection on the platform they are using. Naturally you'll have to identify the customer persona as well, if you haven't done so already. The actual important hypothesis is missing from the statement, and it is a situation you'll run into. Let's ask the team to rephrase the assumption.

They came up with the following:

If we offer 6 plans to our persona (platinum, gold, and silver each with two deductibles), we will be better off than what we have today.

Okay, now we're getting somewhere, although we could invest an effort in defining what "better off" means.

Remember, we already have plans in place anyway, so our hypothesis can be a comparison between the product offerings as we always done it to an offering that is limited to six plans. Naturally we can conduct A/B testing in software to get accurate results, but what if we don't want to invest in software, as the VP is not inclined to give us any resources. We create a mockup and head to the nearest mall. We can screen participants in our small experiment to the persona that we identified and show 10 participants a screenshot of the current system and ten others the limited options. We can then ask them a few targeted questions to get their feedback.

As mentioned, teams buckle at the idea of heading out to the mall and validating a hypothesis as a first step towards validating the assumption. All the better: they are questioning two innate organizational beliefs, namely, *we know better than our customers, thus we can't learn anything by interacting with our customer* and *gathering valuable data should be left to professionals, thus by asking 20 people at the mall we can't expect to achieve anything valuable.*

Hacking away at these beliefs is at the foundation of a lean agile transformation.

Best Practice   Remember, initial validations require no software code. They can be completed by a team at a local mall.

We've completed a full year in transformation. Let's move to witness how it works in reality.

Lessons in Building a Corporate Startup

An Educational Company Story

In section two, I shared with you the ideal transformation, depicting a timeline and the realization of the methods over time. Most books we read end there; they offer the sterile synthesis of the best practice and share a success story or two. I feel this is missing the point. I subtitled section three as "the muddy waters of reality" since in truth things never turn out as planned. Even with the best intentions, transformations change. They both impact and are impacted by organizational realities.

Therefore, in the third section of this book, I share with you mini-stories of successes and failures of enterprise lean agile transformations. There are numerous successes and multiple war stories in the journeys to lean agility. None of these transformations is a complete success or an absolute failure and yet some achieved their original goals while others struggled or failed. As I describe these journeys, which are a mix of fiction and reality (although they sound very real because they describe repeatable behavior experienced by many individuals in multiple organizations but should not be compared to any companies and individuals), you will be able to clearly identify patterns and anti-patterns of an enterprise-level agile transformation.

While written as fiction and simplified for the purpose of this book, each of the following stories shares pragmatic advice and experience from the field of lean agile transformation, which you will be able to immediately apply to the area of your responsibility, to your company or business, and even to your family. Each journey is told through the eyes of a persona who is part of this transformation and each highlights one of the "must-haves" of a lean startup corporation. My intent in this section is to illustrate success and failure stories where best intentions meet reality and discuss what we can learn from them.

■ **Tip** As you read the mini-stories, identify the five techniques to succeed, as discussed in section 2. They were

- Define the mission.
- Identify the customer personas.
- Implement prototype MVP and program training.
- Run experiments with customers to validate your hypotheses.
- Pivot or persevere in a build-measure-learn cycle.

How are the five techniques progressing and changing along with the implementation timeline? Has the persona followed the suggested time spent on activities in the first 30 days, the first 90 days, and the first 12 months?

Achieve and Retain Leadership Support

A Big Data Company Story

On a bright and sunny morning, Nancy Bauer had a clear sense that her new job was going to change the world. She was hired to orchestrate agile and lean transformation for a well-established, almost-150-year-old company that owned an unprecedented data set paired with powerful analytics and a well-packaged set of products and services in its domain of business information. The company recently recruited strong leadership who exhibited transformation thinking and new mentality, and believed in the power of enterprise-level lean agility. For the purpose of this story, I will refer to this enterprise as a Big Data Company, or simply BDC.

© Michael Nir 2018
M. Nir, *The Pragmatist's Guide to Corporate Lean Strategy*,
https://doi.org/10.1007/978-1-4842-3537-9_10

At her job interview a month prior, Nancy was impressed by the level of openness and lean agile thinking she observed while talking to multiple future colleagues in a half-day interview. In her mind, the caliber of interviewers reflected the importance that the company was placing on its transformation, and this interview was a clear indication of the leadership support of agility, the open mind of company's leadership, and the company's collaborative atmosphere. In addition to her future boss, who ran a global Project Management Office organization combining software delivery lifecycle (SDLC) management tooling, portfolio management, and the future agile coaching organization that Nancy was supposed to form and lead with multiple future colleagues, Nancy was interviewed by the Chief of Staff to the CEO as well as one of the senior leaders within its IT organization. This showed the company's commitment to its transformation.

All of the interviews Nancy had were less job interviews and more of conversations between like-minded people who understood the organizational tendencies of the changing world and wanted to make a positive difference in delivering products and services that delighted the customers by being innovative, tuned to customer needs, and delivered with quality, flexibility, and speed.

From the business perspective, though, the company was perceived by the media as a low-growth legacy giant, and there was a lot of pressure on the leadership to turn the ship around.

This mix of cultural, staffing, technical, and managerial challenges coming from the legacy environment did not scare Nancy. On the contrary, her professional motto was all about turning challenges into opportunities. In her mind, every challenge described above gave her a chance to influence the organization and get people excited about agile and lean by being able to orchestrate faster, more predictable, and collaborative delivery; by empowering team-level decision making; by motivating employees through self-organization and teamwork; by building modern skillsets and promoting collaborative goal-driven behaviors; by streamlining processes and giving people the tools they need to provide full visibility, alignment, and drive measurable results throughout the organization. There were numerous opportunities to motivate employees, delight customers, and turn the company's reputation around to be perceived as an innovator in lean-agile thinking and business agility.

These were the thoughts that occupied Nancy's mind as she took the long drive to work on her first day of the job. She already felt empowered and well supported. Even though her job had not started yet, she spent the last two weeks actively interviewing agile coaches for her soon-to-be-formed team, in close collaboration with the company's recruiting department. Being a veteran agile coach who walked a long road from a developer, systems analyst, and Scrum Master to an enterprise-level lean and agile coach, with multiple agile transformations under her belt, Nancy felt that she was well equipped to make this agile implementation a huge success. All the prerequisites were in place: solid business, powerful legacy, dedicated employees, strong leadership. Well, what could potentially go wrong? {Reflect on Nancy's plan below- how does it fit with section 2 approach to a lean transformation?}

Week 1. Defining Leadership at All Levels. In her agile rollout roadmap, Nancy identified two immediate goals for her new role to be successful:

1. Establish an open dialog with company leaders.

2. Show early successes of agile transformation to start building trust and gaining support across BDC and with customers.

There were a few steps to accomplish the first goal: identify the leaders and each leader's area of influence, and whether they had prior experience with lean or agile. Nancy spent a few hours doing research: reviewing org charts, talking to people within the organization, and reading the company's blog. As a result of this research, she identified five primary stakeholders:

1. *Brad Ashcroft*, the CEO. Brad was a modern leader in his late forties who came into his leadership role from the trenches throughout corporate ranks and with a consistent success rate. When Brad was appointed into his role, *Forbes* published an article asking why a technology publishing pioneer and innovator like him would want to run a nearly-150-year-old, low-growth company like BDC. Brad believed in the power of data and analytics, and welcomed business agility as a way of delivering faster and an alignment mechanism between business and technology within his company. Brad was supported by his Chief of Staff, Mary, who was a seasoned strategist with an HR background.

2. *Keith Wrigley*, the CTO. Keith was a charismatic IT professional. In the eyes of BDC employees, Keith exemplified leadership. He knew employees by name, valued their contributions, and was open and transparent in his communications. He enjoyed telling stories highlighting his personal experience; these stories were fascinating because he was vulnerable and open, a combination of a mature professional, coach, and mentor. He held frequent and informative technology town halls and was known for delivering hand-written notes to employees to thank them for achieving major milestones or congratulating them on being nominated by their colleagues. Sharp and action-oriented, Keith's Chief of Staff, Rick, was known among employees for being the decision-maker behind multiple recent personnel and org structure changes.

3. *Ruth Morgan* was running a multi-hundred employee data division. For BDC, data was the core of the business. Ruth was a powerful leader who joined BDC from a similar role with their competitor. She knew her area inside and out, and was determined to take the company's data business to a new level. Seeing data as the company's most valuable asset, she was considering ways of exposing this data without losing BDC's competitive advantage in the area. Most of the senior members of the team she inherited had been with the company for over 20 years, combining a wealth of subject matter expertise with solid industry experience. She was a socially responsible community member who often traveled to developing countries to fight hunger and poverty, and was a big supporter of enterprise lean practices.

4. *Amy Jayashree* was a BDC veteran who had been with the company for almost 30 years, directly from college. Her role was figuring out how the company could use its data and analytics to be able to drive into new areas of service for their customers. She was respected as a thoughtful leader who made a career through hard work and dedication. She trusted and empowered leaders in her group to run the business while holding them accountable for the results.

5. The fifth member of the enterprise leadership team, the Chief People Officer, was *Rosemary Livingston*. Rosemary was new to the role but she had all the qualities of a successful professional in this field of management. She was a people person and a no-nonsense individual, soft spoken but listened to, well-organized, and empowered by the CEO. The People organization (a euphemism for an HR department) at BDC was well run, with a health-awareness workshop, leadership development programs, a professional skill training organization, strong leadership in its recruiting function, and a network of business partners supporting divisions. The latter function was weaker than others with some traditionally-minded HR professionals with staffing industry mentality and background. Rosemary herself personally participated in many company events, speaking with employees and making herself aware of their needs and motivations.

Being a lean agile transformation veteran, Nancy was impressed with the caliber of the company's leadership and their openness to innovation. Nancy started by establishing strong relationships with each of them. She introduced herself to each of the leaders and spoke with them about their business goals and challenges ("**What keeps you up at night?**") and aligned her vision for the enterprise-level agile rollout with their thoughts, challenges, and long-term objectives.

As a result of this analysis, Nancy set up individual regular meetings with Keith, Ruth, Amy, and one of Rose's leaders, ranging from bi-weekly to monthly. She also agreed on the monthly updates as part of the CEO staff meetings for the first six months of the lean agile transformation. The first update was supposed to be the lean agile rollout roadmap that she would create based on their inputs and her first month with the company. This part went smoothly; Nancy felt that there was a strong sense of urgency and craving for a positive change with a powerful leading coalition being formed to promote the change. Nancy was already considering compressing her original roadmap given that the organization was so well aligned, positive, and open-minded.

It was not all that rosy and uneventful, though. In the morning of her first day at the job, Nancy's manager, Mario, who has been extremely welcoming and supportive throughout the interviewing and onboarding process, set up a two-hour meeting to present her with her objectives for the first week, first months, and the first quarter. Even though they had multiple conversations about the goals of business agility and organizational objectives prior to Nancy joining BDC, and the direction of these objectives did not come as a surprise to her, the top-down nature of this two-hour meeting with her immediate manager and a predefined set of objectives presented to her came as a surprise. In addition, Mario, who also led the enterprise Project Management Organization, set up daily meetings with her during the first week, expecting a daily progress report. Nancy was not sure at that point whether it was a sign of support or micromanagement, and decided to go with the flow. She needed as much support as she could get with the scope of changes she was about to introduce into the organization.

Nancy was presented with the list of objectives but she felt that she needed to ask some questions and provide feedback instead of blindly committing to them. While responding to this list of objectives, Nancy told Mario that some of the metrics-based targets were unrealistic, such as 30%+ velocity increase for three teams within three months. Given that she was at a time a sole person with a goal of establishing a lean agile practice within a global company from scratch including establishing vision, creating and getting buy-in for a roadmap, budget management, recruiting, and creating early successes by training people on the ground while serving as a Scrum Master for the first pilot teams until they become self-sustainable, Nancy felt that the objectives had to be revisited.

She shared with Mario that the metrics has to be meaningful and address organizational objectives. She also advocated that they had to baseline data before creating any targets. Overall, she believed that the transformation leaders should be trusted with defining initial pace, which they would then complement with meaningful metrics, such as the number and quality of features delivered to the customer, or customer satisfaction via NPS score, surveys, or business metrics (ROI, P&L, etc.)

The two of them had these conversations over the first week of Nancy's employment and decided to "park it" until the first set of measurable data was available. Both Nancy and Mario seemed to be comfortable with this approach. The only expectation, she was not comfortable with, based on her prior experience as a coach, was to "go faster." She shared with Mario how detrimental unrealistic expectations were as related to lean agile transformations, which are essentially "people business" much more than IT business, and the people business is not something that you can rush. Mario seemed to be supportive of this approach.

■ **Tip** I mentioned in the first section that velocity of a team is a vanity metric that is not meaningful for the business because it reflects quantity rather than quality and business relevance. Notice from the description above how Nancy's manager is drawn immediately to such a metric rather than collaborating with Nancy to figure out an outcome metric and the lead indicators that show progress towards it.

In addition, Nancy found out that Ruth had a strong lean experience at her prior company with a specific well-known productivity framework that was implemented there. Ruth implemented lean practices on the operational side, and she wanted Nancy to do the same. This gave Nancy, who came to BDC from a Chief Operating Officer role at a midsize consulting company, an opportunity to dive deeper into BDC operations. At that point, Nancy felt that she could change her original approach to transforming BDC culture: instead of starting a lean agile transformation from IT, she had a rare opportunity to approach this as an agile and lean transformation to address company needs, and start it as an enterprise-level transformation from the very beginning. This later proved to be a powerful first step, supported by the CEO and recognized on the ground.

As a **Week 1 (Discovery Week)** deliverable, Nancy handed her manager a stakeholder map with all the stakeholders she identified, their areas of responsibility and influence, and their role in the future lean agile transformation. Linked to this spreadsheet, she also had a list of their individual pain points and objectives, as well as their individual experience with agile and lean. This simple template proved to be a powerful tool as it helped Nancy visualize the biggest supporters and detractors of the agile transformation, and develop strategies of supporting the goals of the first group and educating the second.

Week 2. Showing Early Results. The second step in Nancy's roadmap was to show early successes. This was imperative for gaining trust with leadership and having them support the transformation.

For that, she collaborated with Mario to identify the most challenged and yet strategically important business teams with which she could start coaching. It turned out that there were several groups within the company who heard about an agile coach joining the organization and were interested in adopting lean agile methods. Nancy selected to start with a large team that was supporting a new compliance product. This was a 23-person highly distributed team with two primary clusters of team members in New Jersey and in Bangalore, India. There was lack of alignment, communication challenges, limited visibility into deliverables and related milestones, and a huge product backlog with hundreds of bugs and insurmountable technical debt. The timelines were business-driven and excluded input from technology teams, which resulted in employee burn-out and significant technical debt. It was an emotionally charged environment of hardworking and knowledgeable people, and it presented an immediate opportunity for Nancy.

The prerequisites for success were all there: high visibility, subject matter expertise, and urgency for change since it was team members who reached out to her directly asking for lean agile coaching. There were some team members who had prior Scrum or Kanban experience. There was strong IT leadership and a knowledgeable product SME on the team. There were major challenges visible at the top of this organization that had to be immediately addressed. Product leadership was forward-looking and supportive. After two initial conversations and observations, Nancy made a decision to designate this team as a pilot lean agile team and measure their progress as a case for transformation in order to start scaling, get budget approvals, and move forward with global changes with this highly distributed organization. If she succeeded with this team, it would show the power of agility.

Nancy shared this approach with the leaders identified during Week 1, and they were highly supportive, and so was Mario. The only concern was that her manager requested that she schedule training for the same week so that she could prove her own value to the organization since she had been there for almost two weeks. Nancy used this opportunity to educate her manager on industry studies and expectations for an enterprise-level transformation and relevant timelines, but Mario was firm: Nancy had to move faster and start showing measurable outcomes as soon as possible.

This was the start of an unsustainable pace for Nancy. She stayed up for two nights and created a two-day agile training curriculum, similar to the content of a standard Certified Scrum Master class. It was a solid basic course, and she intended to iterate on it with her future team, making it more company-specific and polished as she moved forward.

Nancy was also busy recruiting. This was another area where she and her manager disagreed on the "go faster" approach. Mario felt that they needed to hire the coaching team within a month or two; otherwise he felt that they risked losing budget. Nancy felt that the priority should be on hiring people with the right mindset and relevant experience. Luckily, the first Agile Coach to hire was quickly identified. He was knowledgeable and experienced, and he immediately accepted the offer and was excited to start in two weeks. The search continued for two other open positions. One was an agile coaching position with DevOps experience and a strong technical background. The other was for a lean Six Sigma professional to address the operational needs of the organization.

Meanwhile Nancy's first agile training was a big success. The team that was previously demotivated by unrealistic expectations and lack of self-organization was excited about lean agile values and principles of self-organization and value-driven culture. The interactive nature of the training that Nancy developed allowed team members in business and technology to spend time together and get to know each other as partners. In addition, Nancy came up with a concept of internal certification and developed an online test using one of the sophisticated testing tools so that test takers could see custom grading based on their responses, get advice on the topics of opportunity, and retake the test based on the areas they originally struggled with. The test was neither mandatory nor easy but every single person who attended Nancy's training eventually passed it (some trainees had to take it two or three times, but given the reasonably sized and algorithm-driven question bank each time they got new set of questions, so the test was meaningful and never boring). Each person who passed the test received a completion certificate signed by Nancy.

In a weekly IT leadership meeting during the following week, Nancy was pleasantly surprised to receive kudos from both the IT and business leaders of this product team, especially since she herself nominated this team for an internal leadership award for their passion and enthusiasm in the lean agile transition.

During **week 2**, Nancy continued meeting with the key stakeholders of the company. In one of the meetings, she was introduced to Jack Tulipanin, BDC's Chief Security Officer. Jack had a prior successful startup experience and excelled in building forward-looking, high-performance organizations. Thus it was no surprise that BDC security department was an agile and lean organization of 100 individuals, a fairly lean number for a big data company with regulated data responsibilities. Jack asked Nancy to coach his operations teams and to provide advanced training and Q&A session to his leadership, which she started next day. Jack continued to be a strong partner for Nancy going forward, and his organization continued to perform strongly and was well-known as such across the company. Jack and Nancy were well aligned on the agile and lean journey.

Month 1. Fast forward to the end of the month. The lean agile transformation progressed rapidly. The Lean Agile Coach joined her team and the search continued for two other open agile and two lean coaching positions. Nancy started a lean agile community of practice (CoP) and was running weekly office hours and coaching sessions with an increasing demand. She and other agilists were in demand as trainers and coaches, and she was invited to speak in front of multiple groups within the organization. The newly joined coach and Nancy developed multiple training curricula for Scrum Masters and Product Owners, and a value-based introductory course for leaders; they blogged, met with people, traveled to multiple company locations. Everywhere there were great conversations, learnings, and outcomes. With that, the lean agile rollout model matured.

Best Practice Training is crucial in transforming organizations. Make sure that you train leaders, managers, and team members prior to asking them to perform in the new way of work.

In sum, there were three areas that Nancy and Phil, the newly hired coach, concentrated on:

1. **Training, communication, and education:** From leadership transformation training to role-based and lean agile team training, the goal was to get leadership buy-in with mid-level management as well as senior leadership. This included common challenges with mid-level management and related support from the People organization in empowering managers across BDC to serve as change agents and lead their teams in career development while trusting them with decision-making.

2. **Innovation, openness, and the transparency of execution promoted the new culture,** so Nancy and Phil were able to overcome the mid-level management challenge of a lean agile transformation. At the senior level, Nancy took an approach of a monthly communication cadence with each of her five sponsors, as well as with an identified group of stakeholders within the company: regional leaders, influencers within the technology organization, change agents in Content and Analytics organizations, offshore partners, and vendors. It was important to build strong partnerships at the very beginning of the lean agile transformation to ensure its strong foundation.

3. **Agile transformation:** Nancy, who partnered with the first pilot's leaders in creating two agile teams for the original compliance team pilot, transitioned this pilot to Phil, who partnered with the Product side as well as technology, providing coaching, training, and facilitating dialog. The teams were already showing early successes, streamlining their backlog and enhancing automated test practices to allow for rapid delivery. Security teams implementing another agile framework, Kanban, were able to resolve their operational challenges related to the initially missing work-in-process limit, and an additional pilot team was added to the mix with seven more teams requesting immediate support. At this point, the question was whether to move with agile coaching across the organization, product by product and division by division, or to continue the "coaching on demand" approach to choose from the teams who ask for support. This was a mute decision at this point, since demand significantly exceeded capacity.

4. **Lean practices:** Because of legacy challenges and complex business processes, there were significant operational inefficiencies throughout the organization. There was no common understanding of the differences between lean and agile on the business side, but overall, there was a positive perception that lean would help remove operational inefficiencies, enable faster delivery, and empower employees. When Nancy joined, she was presented with a list of seven lean pilots which were identified at a CEO offsite to represent major opportunity areas for the company. Nancy was presented with this list of lean pilots by Mario as part of her Day 1 objectives, and she was able to agree with him that the lean coaching team would start by addressing the first three highest priority areas in two-week increments with a "go/no-go" checkpoint with sponsors in three months if any of these initiatives would take longer than that.

Very soon, Nancy found out that these were organizational-level impediments that were identified for 4-5 years, each of them with prior failed attempts to rectify. Among the three starting objectives, the first was related to customer contract processing and cycle time, the second covered vendor onboarding, and the third was related to one of the global operations areas. Phil did not have expertise in this area or the interest in business operations, so Nancy took responsibility over two first pilots and Mario supported the third while she was partnering with the recruiting team and vendor partners in hiring two lean coaches.

In her work on the first pilot related to customer contract processing streamlining and cycle time reduction, Nancy met two new stakeholders who later became a driving force in enterprise-level agility: Kristin, the Chief Legal Officer and the contract-related lean pilot sponsor, was involved in this initiative hands-on by attending sprint retrospectives, facilitating decision making, and protecting the team from common management challenges; and Natalie, the Product Owner, was one of senior managers from Legal who embraced this role and became one of the most dedicated and team-oriented Product Owners Nancy had ever met. Throughout her career at BDC, Nancy continued to reach out to Kristin and Natalie for their feedback, mentorship, and support of enterprise-level agility.

At the end of her first month with BDC, Nancy was invited to speak at a global technology town hall about agile and lean transformation, along with the company's CTO. The town hall happened at the end of her second month at the company. In her presentation, Nancy was able to use several dozen examples of the success of early transformation initiatives at BDC globally, from the compliance product team's agile transformation to the vendor onboarding cycle time reduction achieved as part of the lean pilot. The two compliance teams were able to reduce their time to production from three months to a single month; both teams deployed to production every sprint and were capable of deploying even more frequently if required by the business.

A 10% cycle time reduction was achieved by the lean operations team (they started using the term "lean pilots" for these lean-agile mini-projects). After her presentations, Nancy received hundreds of positive responses and requests for coaching, operational support, training, and requests to join her team from multiple international BDC locations (India, London, Ireland, Texas, and California).

Leadership was on board, early successes were established and visible, there was a noticeable budget allocated, and senior management was supportive of the transformation. The early goal of leadership support was achieved in a short time. Nancy felt proud of the success she and her mini-team were able to achieve within a multi-thousand-people company over such a short period of time and was ready to scale the transformation.

Six months. Over the next six months, the Lean Agile Transformation team proved once and again that they could deliver. By that time, the team had grown to 10 members, and the agile teams and lean pilots they were coaching achieved consistent measurable success. Not all of them were successful; one of the early lean pilots aiming to improve global operations efficiency was closed due to lack of sponsor engagement and team member availability. In the overwhelming majority, though, the leadership team as well as practitioners on the ground saw the advantages of agile and lean transformations. They were talking about agile and lean culture spreading far outside IT.

Nancy was excited about the early success and pleasantly overwhelmed with leadership alignment, and yet there were several challenges that kept her up at night.

1. Supply vs. Demand: Demand for agile and lean coaching services significantly exceeded their capacity, which created pressure on coaches to provide services and on her to hire fast.

Nancy tried several approaches to resolve this issue. Her coaching team operated as a Scrum team, so they were able to prioritize their work and commit to a sprint boundary. She spent almost 30% of her time partnering with the internal recruiting organization to do hiring. Internal recruiting did not provide any support for hiring consultants, so Nancy had to engage vendor partners herself and manage the hiring pipeline for her three more open positions at the same time. She and her small team reviewed multiple resumes daily, coordinated the interview process using a Kanban board, and managed communications with multiple vendors. This in turn affected their velocity.

For Nancy personally, these activities negatively affected her work-life balance as well. In the end of six months, on her long-awaited week-long vacation in Hawaii, she had to wake up at 3 a.m. every morning to coordinate hiring activities and interview candidates in the East Coast to share the load with the rest of her team. Agile coaches started taking evening interviews with candidates, but the hiring process went slowly, given the allocated budget, enterprise-level practices, and coaching requirements, preferences for full-time internal coaches, out-of-city location of BDC headquarters which was accessible by car only, and overall high bar for the coaches they were hiring.

On top of these challenges, Mario was pushing Nancy to hire the team as soon as possible, threatening to cut her team's budget if hiring did not happen fast enough. He met with Nancy on a weekly basis, requesting constant updates on how many people were interviewed, the outcome of each interview, and blaming her for not being able to hire fast enough. He shared that Keith was extremely upset with the speed of her hiring process and expected her to move faster. This added stress to an already unsustainable pace. Within a month, Nancy was able to hire two lean Six Sigma practitioners with agile expertise for the lean pilots, but the search for enterprise coaches stalled. Nancy asked for additional support from the recruiting team with whom she was able to develop a close partnership, and she received it, but the hiring process was not moving forward as fast as Mario expected.

These hiring activities were happening on top of all another coaching, training, reporting, and communication activities that the team was actively performing. Nancy was acting as a playing coach, staff manager, and a product owner for agile transformation collaborating with other coaches in all agile coaching and lean pilot activities, resolving escalations, removing organizational level impediments, providing hands-on training, and maintaining reporting and communication with leadership. Nancy offered an Agile Leader title to one of her agile coaches, hoping that he would take over the agile coaching practice, but he was not interested. The hiring quest continued.

2. "Not fast enough:" Since Nancy's second month with BDS, Mario was constantly sharing with Nancy that Keith was upset that the lean agile transformation was not moving fast enough and that he felt Nancy was slowing down in the transformation process. Nancy did not get this feedback from Keith directly, but she trusted Mario, who reported to Keith and was meeting with him every week for their one-on-one. This intensity coming from Mario seemed unfair to Nancy. She questioned this presumed slowness to Mario, who responded by accusing her of not being receptive to feedback, so she made the decision to ignore the noise and "do the right thing."

Anti-patterns   Which mistake did Nancy make as related to leadership alignment and stakeholder management? What are the alternatives? What are potential negative outcomes?

While Nancy's motivation was down after her meetings with Mario, it was the people and teams on the ground that made her work worthwhile. She could see the impact, the positive feedback that she and other coaches were receiving from the teams and business stakeholders, the awards she and her team were nominated for—all of it was encouraging. The metrics collected for all the objectives of lean agile transformation—cycle time reduction, business impact, quality, employee satisfaction—were exceeding the objectives established during her first month at BDC.

> **Tip** When you initiate a lean agile transformation, spend extra time on expectation setting. Ensure that the roadmap of the lean agile transformation, including deliverables with related measurements and milestones, are defined as is the process to collect this data. Set regular data reviews and ensure that the format of the reports that you provide meets the expectations of your audience. Ideally, set up an automated report from a lifecycle management tool of your choice.

3. Hiring block: In order to meet rapid hiring requirements, Nancy did several things: she partnered with her peers in Mario's team to initiate an agile and lean meetup, which eventually brought multiple strong employees to the company. The BDC recruiting team became yet again a strong partner in getting this event off the ground. She also started looking for an agile transformation vendor and initiated an RFP to several agile consulting companies. She received proposals from three companies. The proposals were all thoughtful and well presented, but the three-month budget for each of those consultancies was higher than her annual agile transformation budget. Nancy still found two proposals out of three reasonable and spoke with Mario, who was not supportive of the high spend.

Finally, Nancy reached out to her extended network and was able to identify a candidate who was an active member of the agile community and was well-versed in enterprise-level lean agile practices. This candidate passed all four interviews with carefully selected interviewers of different competencies with a high rating. There were some small red flags; one was that he interviewed with Nancy's team while having a proposal from a different company. On the day of the interview, this coach issued an ultimatum, basically saying that he needed a same-day offer from BDC or he would join the other company. Mario, who also interviewed this coach, was supportive; by the end of the interview day, the paperwork was ready to go, but the coach informed Nancy that he already took the offer from the other company. Two months later, he contacted Nancy to share that his role in a new company was limited to training, which was not interesting for him professionally, so he wanted to join BDC, which he did two weeks later after Nancy and Mario prioritized his paperwork with full support from the recruiting team. It is hard to say why they ignored the obvious red flags and thus this new enterprise agile coach joined the team.

> **Anti-patterns** What were the red flags that Mario and Nancy ignored? Why did both of them made a mistake, despite being seasoned managers? How can you avoid similar hiring mistakes? How can you use the techniques I shared previously such as hypothesis validation to avoid hiring mistakes?

One year. About a year into the transformation, Nancy's Scrum-based approach to running a lean agile coaching team started failing. As a Product Owner, she had to prioritize work with her team. Since demand for coaching exceeded supply, she was personally responsible for notifying those whose requests were deprioritized or scheduled for subsequent sprints, with decisions made by Keith and Mario based on organizational needs. Nancy communicated these decisions to requestors. Most of these conversations went well but few of the requestors were unhappy with the prioritization decisions and felt that Nancy's team was unsupportive.

When Nancy found out about this perception, she presented the list of priorities to every leader for their input. She also reached out to Mario for support, and he promised to speak with the stakeholders who were dissatisfied to explain limited bandwidth of the coaching team. Surprisingly, Mario returned back to her and told her that stakeholder satisfaction was her primary responsibility and she had to figure out how to keep her stakeholders happy. He indicated that she had to figure this out or there would be consequences to her job.

Stunned, Nancy did once again the only thing she could think of to meet the demand: she increased her own work time, working 60-70 hours a week. This also meant additional load on the team of coaches and less time for her to support them, which had a negative effect on team morale.

Finally, the aforementioned new agile coach, the one who had the offer from a different employer, turned out to be a mistake. This coach, while well-educated and knowledgeable about agile practices, was negative and constantly complained: other coaches were unsupportive, the teams he coached exhibited old school thinking, and the technology was outdated. Coaching and supporting him, Nancy overlooked the toxic influence this well-versed, friendly, and influential individual had on the rest of the team.

He approached team members with meaningful questions: "Why do we need to collect metrics? Isn't it a sign of distrust? Why would anyone be interested in the measurable results or team members' feedback if there is trust in their coaching abilities? Why is the CTO making decisions? Why do we need a manager on a coaching team? Isn't agile all about self-organization? Why are we expected to drive results? We should be coaches, not practitioners." This approach turned out to be disruptive. Two of the coaches supported the "no metrics, no results" approach, and the team of coaches started drifting apart.

Initially, this coach was hired primarily because of his development background; however, after he provided agile training to the DevOps team, they found it confusing and asked Nancy for another coach on her team to support them. After he started coaching a large program, they requested another coach with a more positive attitude. His peers found his behavior disrespectful and arrogant. Nancy asked this coach whether he would like to move to a single team. After a short time with this team, the coach himself asked to take him off the team because they were not receptive to his coaching. Those instances created reputational risk for the whole team and decreased morale.

The other challenge was OKR-driven mentality. When I discussed objectives and key results in Section I, I indicated that objectives and key results are an effective alignment tool at the enterprise level but are sometimes misused as a performance management tool. This happened at BDC. While the company was excited about OKR implementation, without proper coaching, it did not go well. Mario was an example of a manager who took time to rewrite OKRs that the coaching team came up with and presented them to the team "for their feedback." The feedback session ended up in a heated conversation. Confronted by the coaches, Mario suggested that they "go with the flow." The next day he told Nancy that she and her team need to meet the OKRs; otherwise, he would let her and "her coaches" go. Stunned, Nancy worked around the clock to meet the objectives set by her manager and minimize the damage to her team.

In the midst of these challenges, Nancy's Transformation Team was growing and included experienced as well as junior coaches, lean startup practitioners, change managers, and innovation leaders. Numerous teams were transitioning to agile, multiple organizational impediments were solved, and hundreds of people were trained. Their work was impacting more and more people within the organization, reaching their second-year business agility objectives.

Throughout the company, employees understood the difference between lean, agile, and lean startup, and used the techniques, changing enterprise culture along the way. Via the train-the-trainer classes, the team trained over 600 employees in their role-based and team-based five agile coaching classes. Lean pilots were formed as a framework for solving enterprise-level challenges. Finance was getting onboard with incremental budgeting. Legal was the biggest supporter of end-to-end enterprise-level agility. The BDC execution world has changed.

At that time, agile implementation was successfully scaling to division-level with SAFe (Scaled Agile Framework)-inspired approach and related training for leaders and SAFe programs.

To solve recruiting challenges, Nancy came up with an Agile Champions program, which was targeted at training and empowering global change agents. The first year of the program, which started with a global Agile Champion gathering in Dublin, Ireland, and finished a year later by graduating a group of 20 strong Scrum Masters and Agile Coaches, was a huge success and a great motivation to BDC employees.

Customized lean-agile training for the HR team was a success, with hundreds of BDC human resource professionals embracing the understanding of lean agile culture, environment, values, and agile teams. This supported the lean agile community in aligning on transparency, a vision-driven culture, and self-organizing cross-functional teams. The company was rethinking its rewards and compensation policy from people-based to team-based.

The coaching team that experienced rapid growth in its first year was also getting together and aligning processes, approaches, and motivation. The whole team went on a roadshow and organized an AgileFest in BDC's Boston, MA office, with one day of trade fair-style training, workshops, and games organized in collaboration with Boston-based BDC Scrum Masters and agile practitioners, and the second day of an "open space" unconference. It also had a panel about enterprise lean agility where Nancy was invited to participate along with Jack and Keith. Things seemed to start getting back on track.

Meanwhile, Keith initiated a large-scale transformation program where lean-agile transformation was just one of the initiatives. He appointed the office of his Chief of Staff to run the program. Cindy, who led the program, was a seasoned IT professional and a long-term company employee. Her work had a significant impact on Nancy's team as Cindy and her team were collecting metrics and presenting them to leadership. She was also responsible for vendor relationship management, including the primary IT vendor who was providing most of the IT resources to BDC.

One of the IT vendors sent their Agile Coaches to teams in two of BDC's global locations. These coaches spent several days interviewing BDC lean agile teams and then presented transformation plans on how they would coach them to the next level of agility to their leaders, thus confusing the teams, regional leaders, and clashing their assessment with the work in flight being done by Nancy's team.

Nancy spoke to Mario, asking for support and alignment, but he shared that there were multiple organizational challenges to his team and there was nothing he could do. His only concern was himself; he personally was not looking good, with several departures of his direct reports since he joined BDC and the negative perception of his own leadership skills by some of his peers. He also mentioned that Cindy and her team would be now collecting enterprise agile metrics at Keith's request. Nancy took several attempts to reach out to Keith to clarify the expectations but he was unavailable.

With the lack of support from Mario, Nancy felt that she had no choice but to start looking for a job. She shared with Mario how she felt and the only response he gave her was to inform him when she started looking for a job, and so she did. Luckily, the first job interview was successful, and Nancy announced her departure a month later. After announcing her departure, Nancy found out that Mario never shared her challenges with Keith, who had high respect for her and was ultimately disappointed by her departure. This came a surprise to her, but it was too late.

On a sunny day, almost two years after she joined BDC, Nancy left the office, surrounded by her teammates, colleagues, and members of the teams who were proud of their self-organization and the work they were doing. She knew that they would never go back to the top-down mentality. Her thoughts were bittersweet. She knew that she made a difference and that agile and lean was now a norm at BDC.

On the day she announced her departure, she received hundreds of phone calls, visits, and e-mails from BDC employees around the globe. Ruth invited her to lunch and spoke about her leadership and the positive difference she made. Keith invited her and her family to visit him in his home town. Amy sent her a warm farewell letter, and Cindy stopped by to thank her for collaboration. Jack's team sent her flowers. Mario and the PMO team threw a warm farewell party. Many employees wrote to her stating that they saw her as a role model; they spoke about her leadership, support, how she and her passion for lean, agility, teamwork, alignment, and customer satisfaction changed their lives. And even though she knew that agile and lean would sustain at BDC with the coaching team she built and though she felt proud of the legacy she was leaving behind, this departure surely did not feel like a victory.

■ **Best Practice**   In Section 2 I shared that coaches are needed for the transformation success. In this case study Nancy's failure had much to do with her inability to quickly atttract talent to lead the lean agile transformation. Make sure you are able to answer the potential spike of requests for coaching. Idenitfy internal champions that could support the program.

On her way out, she met Kristin, who hugged her with tears in her eyes and thanked her for changing the company's culture and affecting many lives in a positive way, including her own. Fighting her own tears, Nancy thought, *I wish I knew how to retain my manager's support and set realistic expectations after the initial rapid success. I wish I did not have to leave.* She wondered which mistakes she made led her to that day.

■ **Tip**   Similar to a lean agile transformation, leadership buy-in is easier to gain than to sustain. Take time to think through the opportunities Nancy missed and the mistakes she did in her two-year tenure at BDC. Try to envision a different ending. What if she stayed at BDC? Would she be fired? Further supported? If she stayed, where would the agile transformation go next? What happened with BDC's agile transformation after her departure? Explain your scenario.

Consider the Corporate Culture

A North East Transportation Corporation Story

In business schools, students are taught that successful businesses start with a good business plan. This 10-billion-dollar corporation started from a complete lack of any business planning, calculations, or financial analysis. It started from the passion, caring, and enthusiasm of its founder. Fifty years ago, he wanted to create a transportation company like no other. His brother was a truck driver who spent long, sleepless nights on cross-country trips. He came home exhausted, spent a few hours, and left for another long and tiring trip. Love for his profession? No one would ever suggest it of him or hundreds of his peers. They made living but their salary did not compensate for the lack of safety of driving after sleepless nights, days and sometimes weeks away from the families, and the road rage they frequently became subject to.

For Drew Evans, founder of North East, the goal was not to make money. Unable to drive any vehicles because of his vision impairment, he felt that truck drivers were no different from airplane pilots or sea captains. However,

© Michael Nir 2018
M. Nir, *The Pragmatist's Guide to Corporate Lean Strategy*,
https://doi.org/10.1007/978-1-4842-3537-9_11

the respect for this profession was lacking. Drew made it his life goal to improve it. He had no business education, just natural entrepreneurial qualities and a passion to change the lives of the people in this difficult profession which was important to others. This passion fueled the family-oriented approach of his business. Since he had no initial capital and no education or prior experience to secure bank loans, he reached out to truck driver associations to raise the initial capital.

This was not common in 1960s but his persuasion and enthusiasm allowed Drew to raise the initial capital. It was not yet sufficient to provide salaries to his employees for the first three months he needed to secure initial business, so he recruited his two grown children, their spouses, two nephews, and three nieces. The business started as a family business, and the hard work and passion paid off very soon. Over 50 year later, the company was doing well with over 8,000 employees globally, a respected brand, and loyal employees and customers. Its Net Promoter Score was steadily over 70 (well above average for a company of this size and industry, and remarkable for any company of any industry) and the business was going well with a fleet of new state-of-the-art trucks and vans. The company was expanding to railroad and sea transportation, and wholesale storage globally.

The only problem that the company had was that its technology was outdated and was not able to comply with multiple security laws and regulations, including data security and overall network security. In addition, the systems were slow and the vehicle dispatch logic was not efficient for thousands of transportation vehicles and routes across US as well as globally. The company had a group of talented internal engineers, which had grown since inception from one person to 80 people in its headquarters near their main storage facility in Texas. This group deployed new versions of the dispatch software every three months, an outsourced company managed the back-office systems, and a computer genius in Silicon Valley took care of security issues and hacker attacks as soon as he became aware of them. This was obviously not sufficient for the needs of the rapidly growing company.

Drew Evans, in his late 70s, had not lost his ties with the company. Every now and then he showed up, walked the floors of the massive, largest-in-town building where North East offices were located, and spoke with employees. Rumors claimed he knew each of them by name. Of course, this was completely impossible but he did address everyone he met by name and was never wrong. Drew was the first one who addressed company leadership in their monthly leaders' huddle and suggested that they add a third measure of success to their two values, which remained untouched from the day it was founded: family values, and loyalty to employees and customers. The third value was *speed*. Actually, Drew suggested *sense of urgency* but the company executives felt that it sounded too harsh for a company that had always valued quality and respect over urgency and impersonal approach. With that, they agreed that their outdated IT department was impeding North East's ability to deliver and develop as fast as modern economy demanded, and the decision was made to hire a new, modern-thinking CIO to change things around.

Hiring a New CIO

The company's leadership had no idea where to find a "world class CIO" (Drew Evans' definition of this role, which all of them liked) so their first step was their internal recruiting department. Given the reputation of North East's brand and generous compensation, internal recruitment's function was to vet the best candidates out of a significant pool of applicants eager to work for the company. Things were different with a new CIO, given lack of their experience as head hunters for this caliber of talent. After careful consideration, a decision was made to go with an external agency. A carefully crafted and very detailed job description was send to TalentFirst, a reputable agency providing technical talent to top companies in multiple industries.

The internal recruiting department was surprised when TalentFirst requested that their representative spend a week at North East shadowing multiple functions not limited to IT. North East management did not mind but questioned the reasoning and the value of the time invested. When TalentFirst assured them that there was no additional charge related to it, they agreed.

Emma from TalentFirst spent a whole working week at North East. Everyone expected her to attend meetings within IT department and review project plans but instead she spent time at the coffee machine, chatted with employees in cafeteria, sat next to one of junior software developers for several hours, joined an application deployment call, made a few friends at the recruiting group, congratulated an employee on her 30-year anniversary with the company, and chatted with a new joiner in the parking lot when they were getting into their cars.

All these interactions were completely random and North East executives felt sorry for the time Emma wasted at their company. In the end of the week, Emma surprised them by saying that now she had a persona image of their new CIO. She said that they would be looking for someone who shared company values of caring about employees and customers, work-life balance, someone who was equally inspirational and supportive. She called this type of manager a "multiplier."[1] In addition to a supportive family-oriented mindset, Emma mentioned that this person needed to help North East get back in touch with its customer. Their customers had changed and they needed more speed, more efficiency, and a better dispatching service, which

---

[1] Liz Wiseman, Greg McKeown. *Multipliers: How the Best Leaders Make Everyone Smarter* (New York, NY: HarperCollins, 2010).

would provide lower costs to them and their businesses. New, more complex algorithms, a new system of online orders, and flexibility of route changes and sophisticated navigation would lead to more flexibility, lower costs, higher speed, and overall service quality. Emma's hypothesis was that this would allow the company to add small businesses as a new group of repeatable customers and shorter distance transportation in addition to long-distance orders from large wholesale clients.

Surprised, Drew asked her how she could know the intricacies of his business, which had nothing to do with her profession. Emma explained that she was not an HR professional and not even a recruiter; she was a lean coach hired by TalentFirst to assess their needs. She said that none of these suggestions were her own; she heard them when she spent a few hours listening to the call center calls randomly and talking with employees who felt that the company was not listening well to market needs and not exploring new markets, thus losing business to more modern and technically savvy competitors. Finally, she said, they would not need to invest in this new business. They could just select one specific area and use one of their smaller trucks for local deliveries. This would require some technical work for online ordering and routing, which could be completed within several brief, possibly one- or two-week iterations. It would require minimal investment, primarily the time of their IT personnel and minimal training, but would allow North East executives to validate the assumption that there was a market need the company was not addressing and provide direction for future development. Emma mentioned that she now had a good idea what type of CIO TalentFirst had to look for: someone who had experience validating business hypotheses with customers, someone who embraced a concept of team-based iterative development called agile, practiced "lean startup" techniques of validating assumptions with real customers, and had a prior record of setting clear goals for employees aligned with customer needs.

Best Practice   When hiring leaders for your transformation, do not concentrate on people who have experience in the same industry, as it has been primarily done within the last 20-30 years. Instead, look at those who bring new culture, the culture of empowerment, the culture of starting with the customer, the culture of learning. This track record creates a modern executive rather than years of similar industry experience in a top-down culture.

In less than a month, such a person was found. Emma personally introduced Pat to the North East executive team. Executives could not believe their eyes. Pat was a tall, young, modern-looking woman in her mid-thirties with bright red highlights in her long hair and green eyes which seemed even bigger because of her huge glasses in an orange glossy frame. She wore skinny black jeans and a T-shirt. Executives wanted to know about her prior employment. It was a coffee business, said Pat. In less than one year, she turned it around, resulting in a new coffee chain in Seattle.

A new coffee chain in Seattle? How is that possible? Well, explained Pat, they found a new niche with online app orders for the most upscale organically grown coffee customized to perfection and served in offices of several large companies, starting from a large online retailer whose employees refused to drink any other coffee after they tried theirs. Quality and convenience, mentioned Pat, were the two criteria that these employees wanted, and her company addressed their needs to perfection, from regular orders to automatic reordering and sequencing their deliveries. "What do you know about the transportation industry?" asked the North East executives. "Nothing," said Pat, "but in a month or so I will know more than many of you." This sounded almost insulting.

They asked about her education. It turned out that Pat graduated from MIT, where she got her Ph.D. in Applied Math. Well, this did not sync with the way she looked, or so they thought. They asked what she did in her spare time. She played video games and went ballroom dancing. What else? She also wrote security patches and posted them to her GitHub account. Pat explained that she was passionate about data security and wanted to protect people and businesses from hackers' breaches. "How long would you need to turn our business around?" they asked. "You will see results within several sprints," said Pat, "but only after proper training and goal setting." Then she explained that "sprint" was a term for these two- to four-week iterations she mentioned earlier. They comes from Scrum, one of the agile frameworks, which emphasizes teamwork, clear short-term objectives, alignment with business stakeholders, ongoing customer communication, and short feedback loops.

This all sounded foreign and vague so North East executives were reluctant to risk their reputation, time, and confuse their employees, but Drew turned their minds around. "I trust Pat," he said. "Let's try it out. Worst case scenario, we will lose one to three months developing some apps and trying new ways of diversifying our business. But since all of those are going to be marginal experiments, we won't pose any danger to our core business or disrupt it in any way. Doesn't sound like too much risk. And besides, I started this company risking all my possessions when I took a loan in the full amount of my home and everything else that I owned, because I believed in success. I see the same light in Pat, and I trust her judgment, so I suggest that we try."

■ **Tip** Executive by in is often the way to ensure support for a successful lean agile transformations.

Drew was not the ultimate decision maker, nor would he ever impose his decision, but his voice was trusted and respected, and so the decision was made to give Pat a chance. The only condition was that Pat could not lay off any of North East's current employees. If they did not have skills needed to develop the mobile apps Pat was talking about, she would find a way to train them. People were the core of the North East business, and this should never change.

First Month

To say that the North East staff was surprised to meet Pat is to say nothing. North East was a company of family and traditions, and Pat did not look like any of them. Many employees were wives of truck drivers who were motivated by making positive input into the business. Hundreds of employees stayed with the company throughout their whole careers. They were shocked to meet Pat and did not take her seriously. This seemed to not even slightly bother Pat, who, despite her tight timeline, looked relaxed and curious. She spent a lot of time with marketing department launching some surveys for truck and van drivers, clients, recipients of their cargo, and technicians who serviced company's truck fleet.

In the company headquarters they installed a three-button stand. When employees were leaving company cafeteria, they were supposed to press a green button if they felt their work day was productive, yellow if they felt they could accomplish more, and red if they felt it was a waste of time and effort. When the red button was prevalent, Pat herself spoke informally with employees around the office to find out what impeded their productivity or what else made their day unproductive. Then, similar stations were installed at the mechanics' station and at the parking garage.

Pat continued listening to calls in the call center, spent time discussing pricing strategy, reviewed algorithms driving their navigation and routing software and was astonished how inflexible it was, and spent hours analyzing application monitoring to review whether it conformed to service level agreements (SLAs) defined with their clients. She also worked with the marketing department to launch something that they called the NPS survey and promised to share results with employees along with executive management. Employees observed Pat's behavior with caution, waiting for her to take steps to restructure IT department and affect their lives and well-being.

Samantha, a Senior Programmer responsible for North East dispatch software who had been with the company for over 20 years and progressed from a mailroom clerk to a senior-level IT professional (North East paid for her on-the-job associate degree in computer science), feared for her job security. She felt threatened by Pat and was already envisioning the boredom of an early retirement. On the second week of Pat's appointment, in the elevator she heard two programmers from another group talking to each other whether they were "on the list" and "when was their turn." She dreaded coming up to her floor because she knew what it meant but she had no choice. She was extremely surprised when she found out that her colleagues were talking about something called "lean startup training." She wondered how relevant it was. North East was not a startup, but she was relieved that she could keep her job and decided to stay open minded and hopefully learn new techniques and programming languages.

Surprisingly, the training had nothing to do with programming languages or IT in general. Software developers and testers were mixed with user experience designers, business representatives, and call center employees to learn about making business hypotheses, **rapidly building software prototypes and customized services to validate these ideas with customers, and using the results of these experiments to either "pivot" and try something else when the ideas didn't work or "persevere" and build new products on the hypothesis that were proven with real customers. By the end of the first month, they split into 15 teams of 7-9 employees, each having developers, testers, a user experience designer, and business stakeholders** representing one of the areas of North East business: routing, assigning, dispatching, targeting, servicing, repair and maintenance, customer service, and other relevant areas. Each team was tasked with identifying hypotheses about changes in the area of their accountability, staging experiments, and pivoting or persevering to define the solution(s) that address customer needs, the ones that would benefit employees, and preserve company values.

90 Days

The first 90 days after Pat was appointed the new CIO flew by very fast for Samantha and the other employees involved in the pilot. They ran weekly experiments using a so-called "validation canvas" which consisted of six columns from stating a customer problem to suggesting a hypothesis and then going over three phases of validation, each ending with a conclusion of "pivot" or "persevere." Figure 11-1 presents a validation canvas template similar to the one they were using.

Experiment Number	Problem	Hypothesis	Validation Criteria	Metrics	Pivot or Persevere?
1					
2					
3					███████
Conclusion:			Next Steps:		

Figure 11-1. Validation canvas template: Theme < ... > Team < ... >.

At the end of a week, they met to present their analysis, answer questions, listen to feedback, and all of this informed their next week's experiment. Some experiments were fairly complex and the team felt that they could not be validated in a week. In this case, they had access to lean startup coaches who advised on different ways of breaking a hypothesis into simpler ones that could be validated within one week. One coach was assigned to two to three teams, and the coaching approach was to "build on what was happening," learning and adjusting every day.

The whole approach was extremely flexible. The only mantra they had was to "fall in love with the problem, not the solution." What it meant in real life was that the employees were expected to involve customers in every idea they had, whether they were working on solutions for internal customers, truck drivers, mechanics, back office employees, or the paying clients who used their services. They were supposed to understand their challenges and co-create solutions together.

Tip   Fall in love with the problem, not the solution!

Samantha's team worked on external client base-related solutions. They were one of three teams targeting expansion of North East business in other areas. They were responsible specifically for researching adjacent businesses: small businesses, individual vendors, specific areas of service or industry, or products. During week one, they decided to start with a hypothesis that small business owners would like to use their services locally for deliveries. Their hypothesis was that small business owners lack availability of local deliveries at an affordable price. To validate this hypothesis, they decided to target several types of small businesses: flower shops, cafes, pharmacies. After initial testing with a cardboard model (they learned this was called a low-fidelity prototype), they built a simple mobile app for these clients to schedule deliveries and adopt a pay-per-service model with pricing scaled based on the number of guaranteed deliveries the client would order from them in one month. They also decided to target suburban and rural areas since they were not convinced that the company should compete with on-foot and bicycle-based delivery done in big cities.

They used multiple venues to market their service and get small business excited by it, but the primary marketing means was talking to them. Coached by their assigned lean startup coach, they did not ask the question of "would you buy our services;" instead, they suggested to purchase a service with minimum number of monthly deliveries and pay a fully refundable fee of $100 per business. They made it clear that their threshold was at least 10 businesses within a 50-mile radius; otherwise, they would refund the sign-up fee. In one week over three experiments, they had only three businesses signed up, and the hypothesis was invalidated. They were initially demotivated to see the results, but their coach told them that a failure is a validated learning, and they did not fail, they learned something, and they should proceed to think of the next steps based on the informal conversations they had with potential clients as they were marketing their business and listen to their responses.

Tip   Failing is learning.

The team compared their notes and took a closer look at the results. They noticed that all three local businesses that signed up were flower shops. Most of them had their own delivery vans. During holidays and on Fridays, though, their vans were not sufficient or lacked equipment to deliver fragile flower arrangements. They were willing to pay a premium for the flexibility of delivery if the quality of their fragile goods was guaranteed by the provider. The team decided to pivot and suggest delivery service specifically to flower shops with insured delivery and special containers to ensure that their fragile goods would be delivered without any impact, in addition to climate control that their special delivery trucks already had. They raised the price and change validation criteria to 25%. In the end of the week, they were surprised to see that 33% of local flower shops enthusiastically signed up, and a few were still thinking. In the end of week, they presented their findings and received encouragement and feedback from their peers from other teams, lean startup coaches, executives, and other business stakeholders; everyone was invited to this event, which was called a "demo." At the demo, the advice their team received was to narrow down their findings.

And of course, they did not stop there. They decided to persevere and find out whether this was specific to the suburban area near Columbus, OH that they researched or if they could use their fleet in other states. They researched suburban areas near Austin, TX and Freehold, NJ. Along the way, they made changes to their newly minted but barebones mobile app based on the feedback from prospective customers, and adjusted their pricing model to make it more flexible. They found out that SLA limits were wider for flower shops that got their orders well in advance, if insurance covered all their losses. Subsequently, they increased response times as well as the insurance limit. The team was hoping for a similar result, but they needed another week for this research and their lean startup coach supported the approach. In one more week, the results exceeded their expectations.

The validation canvas that was used is depicted in Figure 11-2.

Experiment Number	Problem	Hypothesis	Validation Criteria	Actual Metrics	Pivot or Persevere?
1	Small businesses lack delivery options at an affordable price	Sign up model with a monthly minimum and convenience of a mobile app will provide the option small business need	10 business within 50 mile radius out of 50	3 out of 50	Pivot
2	Suburban flower shops have delivery shortage during busy seasons for their fragile deliverables	Specialized trucks and vans with climate control that have the contents insured, equipped with a mobile app for easy scheduling	25% of signups or higher	33%	Persevere
3	Suburban flower shops across America are facing delivery challenges during busy seasons	Specialized climate controlled trucks equipped with a mobile app with content insured are in demand across US	25% of signups or higher	39%	
Conclusion:	There is an opportunity with limited competition to use climate-controlled trucks and mini-vans for transportation of insured fragile and high-demand maintenance goods within 50-mile radius from the original location	**Next Steps:**		Start a separate business under an adjacent brand and continue for 3 months until re-evaluation to potentially include other fragile or rare deliverables with seasonal flexibility	

Figure 11-2. Validation canvas: Theme "Expanding Customer Base" Team #1

At the end of their second week, the team presented their results at the weekly review session and then to the executive council, after they incorporated the feedback from their peers and the business stakeholders. As a result, the recommendation made in the validation canvas above was taken into account, and North East started its daughter business, which involved ground transportation of flowers and then expanded it to other fragile goods for small businesses. Within one year, it earned a reputation as a reliable and flexible partner for hundreds of small and medium businesses. At that time, they merged this business with their primary transportation brand and announced that North East started air transportation of fragile and high value merchandise. They added security measures, hired security personnel, and within the first year achieved half a billion dollars in profit, all of this as a result of research that took less than a month.

The results of the other 14 teams varied. One of the teams that researched data suggested creating a web app to connect their large clients with warehouses. For those clients who expressed interest in participating, their IT team created an interactive matching app that allowed them to find cheap and reliable warehousing solutions within seconds. The app was a big hit in the market and was later sold to an Internet giant for $700 million, benefitting North East and their clients, who got platinum privileges and free lifetime services. Another team rebuilt their dispatch system, making it 10 times more efficient while increasing flexibility and response time 3-5 times. The employee satisfaction team came out with skills matrices and training packages for employees, as well as a clear career path for long-term employees and state-of-the-art onboarding progress for new hires at no additional cost for the company. Everyone was astonished by the impact of the lean startup thinking.

Even more surprising, during these 90 days, employees embraced the values of customer interaction, team-based collaboration, quick validation of ideas based on metrics and objective data, and continuous feedback loop. In three years, Pat left the company because, as she said, "there was no more challenge there." The employees and executives were living and breathing new values. "This would never be possible," she said, "if not for their open mind, collaborative thinking, culture of respect, and customer-driven work ethics."

■ **Tip**   Reflect on this mini-story, can you identify the five techniques to succeed, as discussed in section 2. What was the mission of the tranformation? Who were the personas? Which MVPs were implemented? Describe the experiments that were conducted. How did Pat acheive her goals? Review the Lean validation canvas template provided - how can you use it in your organization?

Evangelize Across the Enterprise

An Educational Company Story

Michael had been with a media and publishing company for five years, making steady career progress from a junior business analyst to a senior delivery manager. He was amazed that one person could learn so much in five years, and this made him very grateful to his employer. He took advantage of every opportunity that presented itself and never regretted tough transition times and the necessity to learn a new area of knowledge every year, especially since each new area came with a new skill that he learned, a promotion, and an opportunity to meet new people. Coming from a Java development lead position with a New York City agency, he felt that he built up his skills to learn almost every aspect of the IT profession.

Starting with his current employer as a junior business analyst in 2005 and learning the hard way how to create solid business cases, he assumed a systems analyst role designing IT applications, creating system and architecture diagrams, and defining data flows. He learned UML (Unified Modeling Language) and used European software called Enterprise Architect to create UML diagrams,

© Michael Nir 2018
M. Nir, *The Pragmatist's Guide to Corporate Lean Strategy*,
https://doi.org/10.1007/978-1-4842-3537-9_12

one flowing into another and generating Java code as an output. Because of his prior experience as a Java developer, Michael was able to troubleshoot this code fast and create deployable software within weeks, proving to be a strong individual contributor. Within months, he was promoted to lead a team of business systems analyst globally and became responsible for a group of 12. It was a knowledgeable and hardworking group of people recognized across the enterprise.

Michael felt that he was "at home" leading a group of like-minded individuals and working on the ground as a Business Systems Analyst for a new content management system (CMS) that would change how the enterprise ran its business along with a vendor on the West Coast who developed the CMS. The vendor insisted that the combined project group use a new software approach referred to as Scrum. They even sent several people including Michael to Scrum Master training, and Michael immediately saw the advantage of this new framework. He felt it was the way he had always developed software; he just didn't know the name for it. Suddenly all his prior experience became meaningful in leading him to this profession. The CMS project was delivered with a big success and Michael was sure at that point that he wanted to become a Scrum Master. Unfortunately, in this company, emerging Scrum Masters belonged to a different organization, the Project Management Office.

Project management as a profession was not respected by the organization. Project managers were seen as policemen who were taking notes at meetings and then following up with everyone on tasks and post due items, while people were busy doing their day-to-day work. Most of the project managers had none or limited IT background so engineers did not take them seriously as a competency, while the project managers constantly complained that the organization did not see the value of their profession.

Luckily for Michael, a new Head of PMO was hired, and the situation quickly changed. The new PMO Director, David, was known for building relationships, standing up for his staff, and excellent problem solving skills. In a few months, David gained respect and established open collaboration with other departments within the company. Michael tried to speak with his own manager, who was permanently unavailable between his job-related and personal travel, and after several weeks of trying, decided to approach the new PMO Director on his own.

Michael's observations about David and his positive reputation turned out to be fully accurate in a conversation that Michael had with David the day after he asked for the meeting. David was an attentive listener, he was genuinely interested in Michael's background, appreciative of his diverse IT experience, and was not concerned about Michael's lack of skills as a project manager. He had an open position available and was willing to do an internal transfer following a quick interview process, which was the company policy. He also volunteered to speak with Michael's manager to ensure that he was also supportive of the move, which he was.

In a week, Michael joined the Project Management office as a project manager. David ensured that he took an industry-recognized project management certification before joining, to ensure that his transition was smooth and that other, very experienced project managers on the team would treat him as an equal, rather than a junior colleague. He recognized that Michael was moving from a managerial position to an individual contributor role and saw it as a sign of courage and a proof of Michael's interest in the new profession and his servant leadership attitude. Michael was immensely grateful to his new manager and excited about the new role.

Initially, everything went well, but then the CTO was promoted to a similar role with a parent company. The new CTO came from operations management and knew nothing about IT. Many excellent technologists and talented engineers left the company. One day, David assembled his team and told them that he was moving on to lead PMO in another organization. For Michael, this was very sad news but he wanted to stay with the company because he saw a way to realize his passion in agile software development. Within a year, he convinced several major programs, including the editorial platform, the core of the business, to move to agile, and in six months, it was a huge success.

Despite this progress, the new IT management was uninvolved, bureaucratic, and unsupportive. Seeing no way to move further in organizational agility, Michael decided to look for a new job and sent his resume to a number of companies. He was pleasantly surprised when he received a call from David the next day. David was leading a project management function in a large educational company where Michael sent his resume and their internal recruiter gave him Michael's resume for consideration. Without a second thought, Michael followed up with a call to company's recruiter, who set up an interview the next day.

For his interview, Michael met with David and two others. One of them was David's peer who led the business analysis (BA) function, similar to Michael's prior role at the media company. Dario, the BA manager, was attentive and friendly, and as passionate about agile as Michael was. In addition, Michael was interviewed by Chris, a Harvard University graduate who was one of the senior project managers. Chris was smart, sharp, but stressed and overworked, so Michael made a mental note to look for signs of unsustainable work approach. He did not observe any signs. David was happy at his new job, and Dario mentioned that he had a flexible schedule and was able to spend time with his family, so the job seemed to Michael like a good horizontal move to a company that valued its employees. Michael was also happy to work for an educational company because he taught at his alma mater for a few years and was fond of academia and learning. Everything was coming together for him with this job move. He announced his departure at his media company, created a comprehensive transition plan, and set up a few training and coaching sessions to ensure that his projects and his agile community of practice-related work would progressing well.

However, there was an unexpected twist along the way. David called Michael to share he was being promoted to lead a lean initiative across the company, so Michael would be reporting directly to Dario. Michael felt happy for David and a little bit worried about his own future but once he found out that he would be reporting to Dario, he felt much better; they were equally passionate about agile, and Dario seemed like a really nice pal.

First Days at the New Job

When Michael joined the educational company, he was pleasantly surprised. This New York-based company called A Plus was a test prep pioneer committed to providing a better education to those who lacked initial knowledge and to enhancing their chances of being admitted to college. Michael was awed by the commitment to quality education, availability of relevant knowledge, and accessibility of skill-enhancing information and tutoring. Michael felt that the community-and-education-targeted nature of the company would be a solid foundation for lean agile culture and mindset. He discussed next steps with Dario, who said that he'd rely on Michael's prior experience with his previous employer and proven leadership to drive agility across A Plus. Michael was up to the challenge.

▓ **Best Practice**   Michael was so excited to join a new company that he forgot to ask a number of important questions about the factors that would support or impede his mission of driving lean agility across the enterprise. What are these questions?

First Day

During his first day with A Plus, Michael met with his peers and leaders across the enterprise. He made the following observations: first, the project management team was comprised of *waterfall* project managers who wanted to change and enterprise business analysts who feared any disruption to their jobs because no one made an effort to create a safe environment where they would feel that their jobs were protected, no matter which framework was implemented. Second, the company's strategy was controlled by two forces: directions from the parent company located in Florida and middle management driven by engineering leaders. Third, the PMO team did not have much respect for Dario; they considering him a micromanager who took credit for the successes of his team and blamed the team for failures. They did their best to not expose any issues until they were too late to fix. In sum, the PMO had all signs of a dysfunctional organization.

Michael also found out that he was taking the place of someone who was being let go because of presumed poor performance. Michael was surprised to meet Yuan, a sharp project manager with a solid engineering background who he was about to replace on the project. Yuan was smart, well-educated, hardworking, and devastated about his departure. This was not a pleasant realization for Michael, who found out that the back-office application Yuan's team was building was already six months late, and upon review of Microsoft project plans, he saw little hope of completing the 100-page scope in the extended three months. In addition, the engineering manager who was in charge of the development work was inexperienced and his technical knowledge was limited.

Michael started by building partnerships. He met his peer, Stan, who was tech savvy and friendly, and became his advisor going forward. Stan confirmed that Dario was known for taking credit for others' work. Michael was already aware of this perception but was not concerned about it because he believed in teamwork and was driven by ability to drive change. He should not have overlooked this warning.

Michael was relieved when Dario told him that he was hiring an Agile Coach who was supposed to join in a week. Combined with everything he learned about his job on day 1, though, this career move looked less and less attractive to Michael. However, the bridges were burnt and he decided to concentrate on the back office project and change the trajectory to move in a positive direction.

First Month

During his first month with A Plus, Michael was able to establish good relationships with multiple stakeholders across the company. He found out that the 100-page requirements document contained way more functionality that was needed to launch the new system, and met with the team of business analysts to suggest a MVP for the launch due in three months. He also spent time with business stakeholders in the back office and other relevant functions to find out which functionality was crucial from their standpoint. His intention was to get the immediate risk out of the way so that he would be able to concentrate on his passion of instilling lean-agility across the organization.

Michael also set up introductory meetings with the majority of the organizational leaders to find out who would support building agility to the enterprise. He found out that most of the A Plus divisional leaders were education professionals with strong backgrounds and ties to the industry. While most of them had never heard of agile, lean, Scrum, or Kanban, they were open minded and frustrated by the time it was taking them to get any changes to the company software implemented, not including new or replatformed systems, which took years to get delivered and were outdated before they were completed. Michael saw these leaders as significant supporters of the agile transformation and future drivers of agility. One of these leaders, Greg, was a fast and smart leader, and a huge proponent of agility. Michael immediately created a partnership with Greg in promoting agility across A Plus.

Dario introduced Michael to Trent, his protégé and a career-oriented recent graduate who was brought in by the former Head of PMO as a relative of someone she knew. Trent graduated from Yale with a degree in world poetry, and this was the first real job after a series of freelancing and dog sitting gigs. Trent was smart, personable, and an avid runner. His work responsibility was limited to managing Clarity, the A Plus project management software, to ensure that everyone entered their vacation time and time spent on projects. Dario felt that Trent with his natural curiosity and lack of professional experience combined with ambition would become good support for rolling out agile as a logistical coordinator and a Scrum Master over a period of time.

As a result of this early relationship building, Michael was invited to provide an update on his Business Systems project to the company's CEO and COO, given the state the project was left in by his predecessor. While others might have considered this a terrifying challenge, Michael saw it as an opportunity to explore the level of support he would get from executive management in rolling out lean agility and get their support for the current project. He made a decision that coming up with a feasible delivery plan and limiting MVP would be his opportunity to build trust with two top executives at A Plus.

The update meeting went extremely well, despite the fact that Michael suggested significant reductions to the scope delivered in three months. He brought in numbers that showed that the effort planned for three months was feasible, it was based on historic data, and it addressed all high priority business needs. Executives were impressed that any estimations were based on empirical data and saw that even though only 20% of originally required features would be built, they covered 80% of use cases. At the end of the meeting, both the CEO and COO offered Michael support for the Business Systems project and agile rollout. Michael was energized and challenged by the high expectations from two most senior people within the company who believed in his abilities. Mario, who was part of the meeting, presented the numbers they collected and was very supportive.

■ **Best Practice**   In a safe environment, there is a great value of presenting issues and potential challenges openly to senior executives, as well as providing recommendations on resolving them, such as Michael and Dario did in suggesting scope reduction based on the data collected.

During his first month with the company, Michael witnessed a strange situation with the newly hired Agile Coach. The Agile Coach hired by Dario started and was let go in a few weeks. Michael never fully understood what happened, and he wasn't able to form a collaborative relationship with this coach in such a short period of time. The coach shared that she felt that she was required by Dario to work around the clock, which affected her health and well-being. Dario claimed that the coach had the wrong attitude.

Michael was sad that this did not work out and hoped that a replacement would be hired soon. Instead, Dario suggested that Michael concentrate on coaching, training, and educating Trent, who would be helping with logistics to gain some technical expertise and eventually become a Scrum Master. The work expectations Dario had for Michael were extreme: Michael still had responsibility to deliver a large program that was just getting back into shape and approaching delivery timelines; to prepare all prerequisites for the agile rollout, which they were planning within three months of Michael joining the company; and to coach Trent to become a Scrum Master.

Best Practice When accepting a role of an lean agile coach or agile leader within an organization, consider transitioning any other responsibilities you may have. Otherwise, this time-consuming role will lead to unsustainable work pace or impede your opportunity to be an effective leader. Similarly, when appointing someone within your organization to lead a lean agile transformation, define who this person is delegating their current responsibilities to.

First Year

With full support from the leadership, Dario insisted on a "big bang" approach to agile transformation. Michael whose previous experience with agile transformation was "ground up," was committed to making it work, although he was hoping for a more organic approach. Dario felt that given the state of their engineering organization they did not have time for a "ground up" approach, which would be much slower.

As a result, they worked with engineering leaders to split all engineers into nine teams, assign Scrum Masters and Product Owners (Michael trained all project managers and business analysts as Scrum Masters and Product Owners), and start sprinting. Several people in these competencies left the company for more traditional roles, but the majority stayed and were excited by the changes.

Resistance came from middle management, specifically in engineering. Despite a lot of coaching work related to their new roles, they were not comfortable losing command-and-control functions, and impeded agility by imposing status reviews, requesting Gantt charts, reassigning people from team to team, and giving them multiteam assignments. Dario and Michael both tried to advocate for a more lean agile approach, and over time they achieved mutual respect, but were still far from true partnership.

Trent was a quick learner, and Michael started transitioning some of the training sessions and facilitation to him as they started up the first Scrum and Kanban teams. The drawback for Michael was that his work-life balance became less and less tolerable: he was coaching nine agile teams and resolving impediments, his team grew to nine Scrum Masters and Agile Coaches, and in addition, he spent numerous hours helping Trent as a coach, trainer, and mentor.

At the end of the first year Michael was with A Plus, to acknowledge the positive change in visibility of software delivery, high quality, and employee satisfaction (all continuously measured since the day the new organizational structure was announced), a Lean Agile Center of Excellence was created and Michael was promoted to a Director of Project Management and Agile Practices, reporting to Dario.

Trent asked Michael to assume formal mentorship because he wanted to repeat the same career as him in 5 years. However, this was not necessary. Shortly after Michael's promotion, Dario announced that Trent was promoted into a similar director-level position. He said he made this decision because he wanted to appoint a peer to Michael. Michael was surprised that Dario hadn't asked for his opinion since he had mentored Trent for over a year, but did not say anything because he was happy for Trent.

This was not the only situation when Michael felt lack of respect from Dario. He felt that Dario frequently presented ideas others came up with or the work done by other team members as his own. The team ran multiple team events at the company level to promote innovation and agile thinking (product workshops, hackathons, idea jams) and Dario marketed each of them as his own invention, without giving credit to the team. When Dario presented one of the ideas as "it came to me in my sleep," Michael openly said that it was in fact his idea based on something he did in his past job, which he previously shared with Dario. Dario asked Michael to stay after the meeting. He said that because he was the ultimate leader of the team, all successes were automatically attributed to him, and Michael should support him in preserving this assumption, otherwise he wasn't a good team player and wasn't concerned about how the team was perceived by others. Michael felt ashamed after this conversation and never brought up with topic again, even when Dario continued to take credit for team successes. Michael believed in teamwork and if Dario wanted to represent himself as the whole team, Michael was in support of that.

Meanwhile Dario started ignoring Michael. He said that Michael's meetings with the CEO and COO were no longer necessary and suggested that Michael find a new area to advance agile transformation to. Michael suggested getting non-software teams involved. A new team member, Mory, took the lead on that and started reporting to Trent, who needed to have direct reports in support of his Director status. Mory started working with the marketing team, who adopted agility with enthusiasm.

The major pain point was the middle managers who started questioning the Scrum Master role given the growing agile maturity of the organization. Michael asked Dario to support him in building trust with this group, but Dario's conversations with them did not strengthen this relationship.

■ **Anti-Pattern**   "Big bang" (full reorg), top-down, lean agile transformation fail to address the minds and hearts of middle managers who play important role in any organization. Not building trust with this group is the first sign of failure for lean agile coaching organization.

During this year, the Lean Agile Center of Excellence became highly respected within the organization. The team was awarded a company award for Innovation and Creativity; they were known across the organization, and highly respected. All Scrum Masters except for Mory reported to Michael as a functional manager, and their agile practices were consistent and reflected an agile mindset. Michael was proud of this team, and working closely with Trent, who was becoming an Agile Coach while retaining his Scrum Master role within Dario's organization, which was now marketed as a Lean Agile Center of Excellence.

Trent reported directly to Dario as a peer to Michael. Michael made it a priority to support Trent, who was learning new agile skills, and to be available to him for any questions and support he needed. Trent was an avid runner and so was the company's CEO and he successfully used this opportunity to promote the work he was doing within the Lean Agile Center of Excellence.

Michael shared the successes of his team. Believing in data, he created a holiday video sharing successes of agile transformation in its first year full of numbers, such as a 40% increase in productivity, 25% increase in quality, and 20 % increase in customer satisfaction. Michael himself was astonished at the rapid success of agility at A Plus.

Three More Years

Michael spent three more years at A Plus. These were years full of victories, although they did not come easily. By the end of the second year, 100% of the software delivery organizations were agile (Scrum or Kanban), in addition to multiple lean agile teams, programs, and divisions (such as Marketing) outside of software delivery. This included a total of 15 software teams and multiple non-software teams across the organization.

For the success in working with the marketing team, Trent was nominated for an A Plus parent company award. Michael was surprised because it was all Mory's coaching, but Trent was so genuinely happy that Michael did not question the fairness of this decision. Later, he found out that Trent was nominated by Dario for this award. Even though it seemed unfair, Michael was happy for Trent, who has grown a lot professionally in these few years. He also felt that the time he invested in Trent was paying off. He did not expect anything in return, although he noticed with sadness that Trent took his support for granted. Leaving his house at 5 a.m. to get to the office for a 7 a.m. coaching session with Trent followed by a full workday starting at 9 a.m., Michael sometimes asked himself whether Trent ever felt grateful to him for investing his time and effort in helping him grow, and then stopped himself because he was not doing it for appreciation or gratitude. He genuinely wanted to support Trent, Dario, and promote agility at A Plus. Agility at A Plus was growing and expanding to the parent company and beyond.

At this point, engineering mid-level management became very vocal in questioning whether the organization needed Scrum Masters anymore. Given the maturity of enterprise-level lean agility, they felt that this role could be played by developers. Given the financial challenges that the company experienced, they argued that Scrum Masters were an expense that the company could easily cut. Michael did not receive support from Dario, who simply suggested laying off 50% of the company's Scrum Masters.

One day, Michael thought of a new angle of looking at the Scrum Master role: since their mission was to orchestrate delivery, he suggested rebranding Scrum Masters as delivery managers. This gave additional responsibilities to Scrum Masters while saving their jobs. The goal was to deliver software rather than promote a collaborative and transparent mindset. The days of hackathons, idea jams, and product workshops were gone.

■ **Anti-Pattern**   When I state that it is important to evangelize lean agile transformation across the enterprise, what do I mean? Which group was ignored in a top-down transformation at A Plus? What about the team members and the teams they were assigned to? Name several ways to overcome these deficiencies.

For Michael, this was a difficult time. His hope of restoring the agile mindset had a lot to do with buy-in from the CEO and COO but he had no direct access to either one of them anymore. He was trying to find ways to restore the lean agile mindset despite the tight budget. The company was moving towards digital education, so product lean agility would matter a lot to make it competitive in the market with all of the innovative apps and crowdsourced question banks it was creating.

The opportunity seemed to present itself. Dario announced to Michael and Trent that the company leadership acknowledged the need for change and influence of digital disruption, and the Lean Agile Center of Excellence team was invited to run an executive offsite for the company's leadership. Dario announced that he expected Michael and Trent come up with ideas on how to implement lean startup techniques to product thinking. Trent was not familiar with lean startup, so Michael spent many hours finding articles for prereading, designing product envisioning exercises, and creating templates for the company's leadership to align on next steps. In between, he was educating Trent on lean startup, reviewing books, and sharing ideas. Dario was invited to attend the event and advocated for one more team member to join because they played an integral role in designing the agenda.

The date of the offsite event held in Florida approached. Dario was busy meeting with executives and presenting the ideas, Trent was busy preparing for a marathon, and Michael did most of the groundwork related to the three-day company leadership offsite. One morning, Dario invited Michael to his office to tell that one additional team member was approved. Michael was already celebrating the opportunity in his mind when he heard that Dario decided that he wanted Trent to join him because he was a rising new star.

He said that the decision had been already made but he was open to listening if Michael objected to an opportunity for Trent to take his career to the next level. Michael was devastated by unfairness of this decision but he also felt happy for Trent. He went to see Trent, who was already aware of this news. Michael congratulated Trent, who acknowledged that he felt bad that he was selected and not Michael, who worked numerous nights to prepare for this event. He offered to tell Dario that Michael deserved the right to participate more than him. Obviously, Michael refused. Instead, he started looking for a new job. Agile coaching was a hot skill on the market. In one week, he had five interviews and got five offers. He accepted one of them and left within two weeks. Trent was promoted to his job, and Dario left a year later, leaving Trent in charge of the Lean Agile Center of Excellence.

When Michael announced his departure from A Plus, he told Dario that his decision to select Trent to join him for the executive offsite was a trigger for his decision, and Dario's lack of support was a significant concern of his. Dario acknowledged the situation and said he understood that the decision was unfair given that Michael did the lion's share of the prep work, but that the company's CEO expressed his preference of Trent joining the offsite based on their shared interests in sports and a kayaking activity in the scope of this event. Michael was not sports-oriented, so Dario did not feel like objecting to this request and explaining to CEO who did the actual work. For Michael, this was just another confirmation that his manager did not support him, so he felt confident in his decision to leave.

Best Practice   Was Michael's coaching time at A Plus a success or a failure? Did he manage to transform the organization? How was this transformation for him personally? Despite all the hard work, Michael did not succeed from a career perspective. What could have he done differently in building his relationships within the management team and with his immediate manager?

Agility at A Plus did not disappear. It was already in a steady state with the team strong enough to sustain agility across the enterprise. There could be no better acknowledgement to the work that Agile Center of Excellence had done. If Dario and Michael stayed with the company, though, the next step would have been to emphasize agile prioritization to build 20% of features to support 80% of the functionality required, establish a build-measure-learn loop for any product they were building, and implement lean startup thinking at the enterprise level. Up until now, agile product portfolio management was a challenge for A Plus.

Best Practice   Many companies face a dilemma of whether to hire Agile Coaches externally or to implement an Agile Center of Excellence within the company. The most successful implementations combine both: a strong team of external coaches and internal Center of Excellence as a heart of an enterprise-wide agile implementation.

What Big Data Doesn't Tell Us

According to big data, as Seth Stephens-Davidowitz tells us in *Everybody Lies*,[1] only 9% of readers read the summary of a book, so why bother? I was sharing this nugget of information with my spouse as I was reluctantly contemplating how to end this book. She was incredulous; surely this piece of information is false, she claimed. During her writing of a PhD thesis in urban planning, she and her fellow doctorate students always flipped to the summary of a book or research to analyze the merits of the information.

Upon further pondering, I think I know where the discrepancy is. Big data analyzes the reading patterns of e-books, books in digital format, and one can only assume that flipping to the summary of a print book is much easier than scrolling to the ending of an e-book. Match that with reading patterns of print vs. digital books and you might conclude that the 9% mentioned above is quite misleading;[2] actually many readers might be flipping to the end of the book to read whether the author is worth his salt. On top of which, big data still doesn't tell us who those 9% might be; maybe they are the most esteemed leaders of society? So here I am writing the summary.

---

[1] Seth Stephens-Davidowitz, *Everybody Lies: Big Data, New Data, and What the Internet Can Tell Us About Who We Really Are* (New York, NY: Dey Street Books, 2017).

[2] According to a PEW research report from 2016, while the number of e-books is on the rise, print books remain a much more popular format. www.pewinternet.org/2016/09/01/book-reading-2016/.

© Michael Nir 2018
M. Nir, *The Pragmatist's Guide to Corporate Lean Strategy*,
https://doi.org/10.1007/978-1-4842-3537-9_13

There's more than meets the eyes in the research above, since as we become increasingly reliant on data and enamored with the BIG kind, we might be missing the forest for the trees in three aspects, specifically

- We fail to empathize with our consumers;
- We lose the forest for the trees;
- We are bound to the data we observe and measure.

We fail to empathize with our consumers: I started this book with a story about lean implementation in a color-coating manufacturing line. What I omitted is that we had data; we had lots and lots of data. As industrial engineers we were taught that we'll find the answer in the data. The three of us sifted through 13 spreadsheet files detailing two years' worth of production times. We analyzed them by every means an engineer can think of: filtering, sorting, statistical analysis, pivot tables, pivot charts, VBA macros, and nada. We couldn't find the solution. The data measured outputs and we were interested in impacts. While the data was a first necessary step, it was a partial solution. We had to observe the process to gain the necessary insights. We had to spend day and night shifts with the employees; drink dark roasted coffee, no cream, no sugar, seven times boiled, with them; observe their behavior during the breaks; and notice the patterns of effort and speed. The data doesn't tell us this story; the consumers do. Starting with the customer in mind is key. Accordingly, that was my first chapter. Lean thinking starts with empathizing with the consumer, and that's something data can't offer.

We lose the forest for the trees: During the same trip to Helsingborg, Sweden where I met Henrik Kniberg, I also had the opportunity to sit through Douglas Hubbard's talk where he explained how to measure anything.[3] What struck me the most wasn't that we could measure anything that we wanted; rather, it was that the measurements we focus on often measure what we already know and don't provide much value. As this was a project management conference, he shared his research demonstrating that the indicators we often monitor for predicting the success of a project were misleading. While the accurate indicator for project success was measured, it was lost in the vast amount of data we were accumulating! The concept was both innovative and stimulating, and it complemented a book I released previously that year. In *The Agile PMO*,[4] I describe how project management offices often invest inordinate effort in managing non-value-driven tasks. They encumber the organization with tools, techniques, and templates that are obstructing the delivery of value.

---

[3]Douglas Hubbard, *How to Measure Anything: Finding the Value of Intangibles in Business* 3rd Edition (Hoboken, NJ: Wiley, 2014).
[4]Michael Nir, *The Agile PMO: Leading the Effective, Value Driven, Project Management Office* (Boston, MA: Sapir Publishing, 2014).

They require compliance to impractical duration, cost estimating and time reporting in order to measure progress against the plan. However, Douglas Hubbard demonstrated that not only are PMOs wasteful, they also have little impact on project success. In this book, you notice this recurring pattern of waste. Too much data is waste. We are limited by our ability to analyze data and it often stands in the way of truly understanding where we are and where we're heading.

We are bound to the data we observe and measure: Daniel Kahneman's *Thinking Fast and Slow* describes a concept called *WYSIATI—What You See Is All There Is.* He continues to explain[5] that *WYSIATI means that we use the information we have as if it is the only information. We don't spend much time saying, "Well, there is much we don't know." We make do with what we do know. And that concept is very central to the functioning of our mind.* In other words, the data we measure provides an answer to what we were looking for in the first place. We are searching under the light rather than asking how big the area is outside the light. The user experience, product, and engineering team that was developing a new editor based on the surveys from the consumers and the feedback from marketing and operations was doing as they were told; they created a rich, customizable, feature-full solution based on the data that was analyzed. However, the data didn't tell the story of what users really needed, which was a fast and simple-to-use editor, since it wasn't what they were looking for in the first place. Another famous Daniel, Daniel Gilbert, a Harvard College Professor of Psychology at Harvard University, discusses the challenge in a famous TED talk and in his book[6]; people play the lottery since they see all the winners. They are oblivious to the losers.[7] My niece wants to pursue a career in singing because she is infatuated with the success of her favorite singer without asking how many failed along the way. At the airport, the bookstands display successful businessman selling their secrets of success. However, how many have followed the same secret advice and never reached the airport bookstand? Thus, data tells us a skewed story, a partial story, rather than complete story, the story that's hidden from sight. Of course, this isn't the fault of the data, but the fault of the questions we are asking and the blind conviction with which we are treating it.

In this book, the idea that *more is not better* is a thread implicitly presented. In the introduction, I discussed my favorite microwave example. The device with more buttons doesn't make it a better product; on the contrary, it makes it burdensome and complex. The various assumptions we might have concerning the product, market, and users are not validated. These are the

---

[5]*Monitor on Psychology*, Lea Winerman interview with Professor Daniel Kahneman, "A machine for jumping to conclusions," February, 2012.
[6]Daniel Gilbert, *Stumbling on Happiness* (New York, NY: Vintage, 2007).
[7]This is sometimes referred to as the survivalist bias.

same assumptions that are collected before the product is authorized by senior executives and are captured by the business analyst in page three of the marketing requirement document but are never revisited later. Rather than iteratively creating small releases of the product based on the assumptions and validating them with consumer feedback, the product is created "big bang" style and more often than not fails.

In the introduction, I explained that while many books have been written on lean, agile, design thinking, disciplined delivery, scaled agile, and lean user experience, we are missing the business agility driver and the unified engine integrating them to a single delivery model in the enterprise. I further described this in the first section, which illustrated the limits of the various methods and the tweaks and adaptations I made when scaling them to big businesses. The first chapter in this section explained that starting with the customer in mind is easier said than done. Inside-out thinking rules in organizations. Employees hide behind mounds of data, yielding them proficiently to fight back any suggestion regarding direct feedback from the consumer, while in truth they are terrified of that exact direct interaction with users, internal and external. I offered best practices to circumvent this fear and suggested the usage of a living persona that is constantly refined to pull the entrenched employees to interact with users. In the second chapter, I introduced objectives and key results (OKRs) as a mechanism to focus on a small number of objectives and collecting the right data that supports them. That is contrary to the many top-down KPIs that often organizations collect that hardly support the transformation. It is also an example of how too much data stands in the way of achieving the vision we set out to accomplish. In the third chapter, I described the myriad frameworks that organizations have in place, yet many are operating in a silo, not aligned with business outcomes and disconnected from one another. Once again, there's a lot of data, but the value is not in more data; rather, it is in identifying and synthesizing an integrative operating model. The fourth chapter of section one discussed the challenges I had when introducing the concepts of vanity metrics and validated learning in enterprises. We are convinced that if we could measure and report just one more thing about anything, our results will improve. Measurement drives behavior; however is this the behavior we are trying to achieve? In agile implementation, executives are blinded by measuring teams' velocity; that's indeed more data but it yields the wrong metric and leads to bad team behavior and gaming the system. In the fifth and last chapter of the first section, I presented the lean startup concept of pivot or persevere. Enterprises fear pivoting. Once a project is approved, or a product is developed, it is very hard to kill it. Actually, the traditional data collection mechanisms that the enterprise puts in place are such that support the completion of the endeavour. Hardly ever does the data that we select to collect undermine the effort itself. In the rare occurrence that the data points to pivoting, the decision makers either ask for more data rather than act on what they have or ignore the data altogether.

The three chapters of part 2 described a framework, not a one-size-fit-all methodology, providing a set of tools and techniques with well-defined values and best practices while retaining the flexibility of implementation. The section focused on the transformation steps of the first 30 days, the first 90 days, and the first 12 months; it provided guidelines for rapid implementation. Success is based on the ability to move from long-held beliefs of central, data-driven decision making to embracing a local, lean agile team where decisions are based on feedback from the customer. The three case studies in section three told the same story: a lean agile transformation is about getting the organization to test small and respond quickly.

There's nothing inherently wrong with collecting a lot data; rather it is our ability to comprehend and analyze large volumes of it, as well as the fact that the more you invest in collecting it, the more you are committed to it. This was already evident to me in 2005 when I was working as a program budget and schedule controller at a facility turnaround of a petrochemical plant. We were tasked with producing huge Gantt charts initially using Microsoft Project® and later on Primavera®. The 4,000 tasks in the schedule plan were of little use to the managers and I noticed that any plan that was more than 30 task entries was useless. The quest to identify and monitor every 6-hour-long activity of the 30-day petrochemical process plant turnaround was futile; more was less. The same phenomena occurred later at a medical device manufacturing plant where I was introduced to the NP complex problem of scheduling.[8] Planning the sequence of parts to production was tricky; identifying the sequencing of the 75 plastic extruders and timing the production with the downstream assembly lines was next to impossible. I was consulting the vice president of operations; however, I wasn't able to dissuade him from investing $525,000 to purchase software to optimize the scheduling process. A year later, scheduling software in place, the five manufacturing engineers spent three days once a month configuring the software with the data to generate production plans. The only problem was that a day into the cycle of the new plan, something would go wrong, a machine would break down, and the plan would go out the window.

This is not new. In *Lean Thinking: Banish Waste and Create Wealth in Your Corporation*, authors Womack and Jones[9] describe the same pattern in production facilities: executives invest in the best and most expensive automatic production machine and software only to find out that it limits production flexibility and response time to the market. When faced with

---

[8]Michael Nir, *Agile Decisions: Driving Effective Agile Decisions in Business*, (Boston, MA: Sapir Publishing, 2014).
[9]James P. Womack and Daniel T. Jones, *Lean Thinking: Banish Waste and Create Wealth in Your Corporation, Revised and Updated* (New York, NY: Productivity Press, 2003).

changing market conditions, more is less. The same problem is exposed in product management: running numerous focus groups, sending survey upon survey, gathering more and more data, yet unable to act upon it in a timely manner. Sometimes this is referred to as analysis paralysis.

More data isn't bad in itself; our ability to act upon it is the challenge and the tendency to delay decisions and create larger and larger solutions. In that sense, lean agile enables local, relatively cheap, quick decisions. When the decisions are wrong, the impact is minimal.

To recap, I'd like to revisit the example of how a healthcare provider used the approach to strategize and execute the replacement of a policy administration back-end system it had in place for 50 years. Similar, costly replacement projects are everywhere and are often late in delivery, cost more than expected, with users hardly ever happy with the results. The system they had in place was outdated, overdue for change, and not able to support the consumer experience the company wanted to provide. Traditionally, these projects commence with a long stage of requirement gathering done through workshops, job shadowing, and interviews. The requirement document is extensive, there's too much data that all too often both captures the legacy thinking that has been around the company for decades as well as lists numerous exceptions that occur rarely. The team created a synergetic unified delivery model and then used lean agile methods to identify the most important system elements that they then put in place, released internally, and received customer feedback on. Then they iteratively added new products and migrated existing ones based on discussions with the product, operations, marketing, and sales teams.

One might argue that since they replaced a legacy system, the full scope of functionality was predetermined. However, they learned that many existing legacy features were obsolete; others were developed in the past, taking into account legacy constraints that needed to be revisited; and yet others were based on regulatory interpretations that could be reassessed. These features would have found themselves part of the new system if the team followed the traditional approach to requirement gathering and project management. However, following lean agile principles, the team was able to shave off half of the normal forecasted duration, reduce cost, and, most importantly, deliver a system that was in line with the future vision rather than capturing legacy thinking.

Afterwards: Your Next Steps

In this book, I shared both theory and its application in practice. While these case studies have a lot in common, the outcome is predefined. Theoretical knowledge is important and provides the foundation; however, actual success depends on an open mind, respect, and a customer-driven culture. I hope that best practices described in this book provide practical steps for you to follow, while red flags experienced by its characters will provide examples of a "bad smell," signs of caution that should keep you as a transformation stakeholder up at night and indicate that there is some work for you to do in order to make this transformation a complete success that will be sustained in the organization whether you are there in person or not.

What are your next steps? I suggest the three-step approach:

1. **Assess the level of your organizational lean agility.** Answer the questions: Is ongoing feedback collected from the customers? How does the company respond to it? What is the level of employee involvement in the build-measure-learn loop?

2. Based on the results, **devise the 90-day plan**. What are the prerequisites? What training is needed? Who is capable of providing this type of training? Is there a need for external trainers and coaches? Is the culture open to the change? Does the organizational structure and skillset support design sprints[10] with rapid prototyping? Does the enterprise culture promote open minds and customer-driven thinking?

3. **Start executing on your 90-day plan**; adjust as required by your organizational culture and success of early experiments. As you approach the end of the first months, start planning for 120 days and progressively at least 90 days ahead with high-level annual and quarterly goals transparent across the enterprise. Measure early successes, address challenges, and "build on what is happening" using the tips and tricks described in this book.

I wish you success on every step of this journey.

---

[10]Jake Knapp, John Zeratsky, Braden Kowitz, *Sprint: How to Solve Big Problems and Test New Ideas in Just Five Days* (New York, NY: Simon & Schuster, 2016).

I

Index

© Michael Nir 2018
M. Nir, *The Pragmatist's Guide to Corporate Lean Strategy*,
https://doi.org/10.1007/978-1-4842-3537-9

Get the eBook for only $5!

Why limit yourself?

With most of our titles available in both PDF and ePUB format, you can access your content wherever and however you wish—on your PC, phone, tablet, or reader.

Since you've purchased this print book, we are happy to offer you the eBook for just $5.

To learn more, go to http://www.apress.com/companion or contact support@apress.com.

Apress®

CPSIA information can be obtained
at www.ICGtesting.com
Printed in the USA
LVOW13s1616170418
573810LV00003B/5/P

9 781484 235362